Other books by Michelle Hamilton:

I Would Still Be Drowned In Tears: Spiritualism in the
     Lincoln White House

My Heart Is In The Cause: The Civil War Diaries of Private
     James A. Meyers

Civil War Ghosts

# HAUNTED LAND

## Ghosts, Witches, and Divination in the 18th Century

Michelle Hamilton

Michelle Hamilton

# Haunted Land

*First Edition:*
First printing

# Michelle Hamilton

PUBLISHED BY HAUNTED ROAD MEDIA, LLC
www.hauntedroadmedia.com

United States of America

For Mom and Dad

Michelle Hamilton

# Acknowledgments

I would like to thank the following individuals:

This project would not have been completed without the love and support of my parents. Momand Dad, I love you.

I want to thank my co-workers at the Mary Washington House and the Washington Heritage Museums. You all kept me sane this year.

Thanks also must be given to my poodles, Belle and Violet, their cuddles and love made this year bearable.

Finally, I want to thank Mike Ricksecker and Haunted Road Media for their continued support.

# Michelle Hamilton

# Table of Contents

Michelle Hamilton

# Introduction

The 18th-century is one of the most fascinating and complex eras in history. It was an era of enlightenment and revolution. New innovations in science and manufacturing improved the lives of millions. A band of committed patriots in the American colonies sparked a revolution that defeated the world's largest empire. It was an era that helped usher in the modern world.

But it was also an era were the belief in witches, ghosts, and sorcery was prevalent. The belief in supernatural forces stood in contrast with enlightenment thinking, which embraced a more rational view of the world backed by scientific study and experimentation. This conflict between old world thinking and the enlightenment played out in the popular press of the 18th-century in both England and its American colonies.

Newspapers were extremely popular in the 18th-century as literacy rates were growing and colonists were eager to follow the latest news and fashion from England. Most of the articles reprinted in this collection were originally printed in English newspapers and were then reprinted in American papers. These articles present a window into 18th-century views on the paranormal.

The articles featured in this study present a society at conflict with itself—a conflict between rational thought and traditional beliefs. The common people in England and the colonies held fast to the belief in ghosts and witchcraft. These beliefs helped them to make sense of the world around them and helped kept the world ordered. If the crops failed or a healthy young woman suddenly fell ill with a deadly disease, it had to be caused by supernatural forces. A witch had to be responsible and he or she had to be punished to stop the misfortune and bring order back to the community.

At the same time, enlightenment thinking was changing how the world was viewed by the educated elite. Universities and colleges in England and the colonies introduced the writings of philosophers and scientist who challenged the belief in the paranormal to the sons of the wealthy. What was once believed to be the result of witchcraft was shown to have natural origins. In 1735 as part of the enlightenment, England's parliament passed the Witchcraft Act which made it a crime for a person to accuse another of having magical powers or of being a witch. The act ended the legal hunting and executions of suspected witches. Though the persecution of suspected witches continued in both England and America throughout the 1700s.

Despite the progressive legislation such as the Witchcraft Act of 1735, traditional beliefs persisted. Witches were still blamed for any misfortune, fortune tellers and conjurors were consulted for advice, and the ghosts of murder victims stalked the streets—much to the disdain of the newspaper editors who covered these stories.

The 18th-century was an era of political and social instability. During most of the century England was at war either on the continent of Europe or in the New World. This political instability is reflected in the reports of the paranormal. Ghosts, witches, and fortune tellers appeared frequently in the pages of newspapers following periods of armed conflict and political instability. The most dramatic is the period after the American Revolution.

These accounts featured in this work occurred during the period that created this nation. Interest in the paranormal has been ingrained in our culture from its very founding as a British colony. The recent embrace of all things that go bump in the night is not a recent phenomenon as the following accounts show.

Studies of the paranormal tend to focus on the 19th-century with the birth of the Spiritualist movement in 1848 in the United States and the beginning of paranormal research with the creation of the Ghost Club in 1862 and the Society for Paranormal Research in 1882 in England. The 18th-century is largely overlooked and is characterized as a rational era sandwiched between the excess of the witch hunting craze of the 16th and 17th centuries and the emergence of Spiritualism in the 19th-century. This work attempts to shed some light on the paranormal in the 18th-century and give this period its due study.

Settle in your favorite reading chair and pour yourself a drink and be prepared to meet restless ghosts, witches, and conjurers. I hope you come away with a fresh appraisal of the era.

# Chapter I

## Ghosts

Ghosts have been seen since the dawn of time. The earliest ghost story dates from ancient Greece and was recounted by the Roman writer Pliny the Younger around 100 AD. Pliny recounted the story of a house in Athens, Greece that was haunted by the ghost of an emaciated old man who rattled chains that were wrapped around his hands and feet. The haunting caused the previous owners to descend into madness and the mansion was abandoned.

The house was sold to a philosopher named Athenodorus who happily moved into his new home despite knowing the history of the house. On his first night in the mansion, Athenodorus made himself comfortable with his work and sent his servants away. As the evening wore on, the sounds of moaning and the rattling of chains were heard. Athenodorus ignored the sounds and continued working. The noise came closer and closer, but Athenodorus would not be disturbed. The ghost of the old man then entered

Athenodorus's room. The philosopher finally looked up from his work and acknowledged the specter.

The ghost beckoned Athenodorus to follow him. But the philosopher did not want to be disturbed and returned to his work. The frustrated ghost rattled his chains angerly until Athenodorus followed the old man into the courtyard. After pointing at a location, the specter dissolved. Athenodorus marked the location that the ghost disappeared had indicated and the next morning had the magistrates dig at that location. They discovered the skeletal remains of a man wrapped in chains. The bones had been there for a long time. The remains were collected and given a proper burial. The ghost of the old man was appeased, and he did not haunt the mansion again.

The story of Athenodorus's haunted mansion firmly established the trope of the restless spirit that needed to be appeased following some grave injustice. This trope would continue into the 18th-century, as the following accounts illustrate. Bellow you will meet the restless spirits of murder victims crying out for justice. Also, in the true spirit of the enlightenment you will meet clever spirits that are more than what they appear on the surface.

## *The Pennsylvania Gazette,* Philadelphia, Pennsylvania, December 16-23, 1729, pg. 3.

*Boston, Decemb.* 1.

Last week one — belonging to Ipswich came to this Place, and related, That some Time since he was at Canso in Nova Scotia, and that on a certain Day there appeared to him an Apparition wounded and bloody, and told him that he was such a Person, telling his Name, and that at such a Time and Place, mentioning both, he was murdered by one — who was at Rhode Island, and desired him to go to the said Person, and charge him with the said Murder, and prosecute him there, naming several Circumstances and Things relating to the Murder; and that since his Arrival from Canso to Ipswich, the said Apparition had appeared to him again, and urged him immediately to prosecute the said Affair. The abovesaid Person having related the Matter, was advised and encouraged to go to Rhode-Island, and engage therein, and he accordingly set out for that Place on Thursday last.

## *The Virginia Gazette*, Williamsburg, Virginia, June 3-10, 1737, pg. 4.

*Williamsburg June* 10.

We hear also, from *Hanover* County, That one William Marr,[1] a Servant of Col. *John Chiswell's*,[2] came from his said Master's, to the Court-house on Saturday last, and inform'd [informed] the King's Deputy-Attorney,[3] that he was

---

[1] William Marr was an indentured servant owned by Charles and John Chiswell in Hanover County, Virginia. Marr ran away from Chiswell's property in January 1736. Shortly after Marr's disappearance, Charles Chiswell posted a reward notice for his servant: "*RAN away, last* January, *from* Charles Chiswell, *Esq; of* Hanover *County, a Servant Man, nam'd* [named] William Marr, *an* Irishman, *aged about* 30, *of a middle Stature, and a brown Complextion. He wore a Kersey Coat, with Mettal Buttons. He cros'd* [crossed] *over* Potomack, *on the Ice, below* Ockoquan [Occoquan], *and hath been seen in* Maryland." (*The Virginia Gazette*, Williamsburg, Virginia, February 18-25, 1736, pg. 4). Chiswell offered a reward of twenty shillings for Marr's apprehension.

[2] John Chiswell (c.1710-1766) was a prominent plantation owner and member of the House of Burgesses. In 1766, Chiswell committed suicide after murdering Robert Routledge in a tavern brawl.

[3] In colonial Virginia, the King's Deputy Attorney was a predecessor of the District Attorney.

concern'd [concerned] in the Murder of a Man; upon which he took him before *Robert Lewis*,[4] and *Richard Clough*, Gent. [gentlemen] Two of his Majesty's Justices of that County, where he voluntarily confess'd [confessed] as fallows: That he ran away some Time ago, and joyn'd [joined] in Company with 3 other Servants, viz. Peter Heckie, Matthew O'Conner, and Bryan Conner, belonging to Capt. Avery, and his Son, of *Prince William* County, who were also ran away from their Masters; that he the said Marr, and the 3 other Servants, went far back in the Woods, and on the last Day of April, they came to a Cabbin near Great Cape Capon Creek, in *Orange* County, in which was one Lifelet Larby, (a Person who liv'd [lived] by Hunting) and after staying all Night with him, and being entertain'd [entertained] as well as cou'd [could] be expected in such a Place, the said Lifelet Larby having Occasion to go down among the Inhabitants, to buy Powder and Shot, he set out the next Day, and the said 4 Men with him, in seeming Friendship, about 250 Yards, and they suspecting the said Larby wou'd [would] discover to the Inhabitants where the said Runaways were, one them propos'd [proposed] killing him, and it being consented to by the rest, Peter Heckie, the first Proposer, shot the said Lifelet Larby thro' [through] the Back with a Gun of the said Lifelet's, and afterwards beat his Brains out with the But End thereof, and went away, leaving him in that Condition. That the said Marr being very uneasy in his Mind that he had consented to such a barbarous Murder, and being also apprehensive that the other 3 who were all Ship-Mates, and he a Stranger to them, might kill him too, took the first Opportunity to leave them, and accordingly did, but being taken up in the lower Parts of *Orange* County, was sent from Constable to Constable to his late Master's

---

[4] Robert Lewis of Granvil (c. 1739-c. 1780).

House. He having a Remorse of Conscience, and being terrify'd [terrified] (as he says) by the Apparition of the murder'd [murdered] Man, he cou'd [could] not rest till be discover'd [discovered] the Murder, and accordingly came to the Court house this Day, and made his Information and Confession, (which the above is the Substance of) which he sign'd [signed], and was thereupon committed to the Goal [jail] of that County, in order for a further Examination.

He gives, a frightful Account of the Apparition of the murder'd [murdered] Man's tormenting him; which seems incredible, and as if the Man was out of his Senses; but that the Circumstances of his whole Account of the Fact, the Pertinancy of his Answers, and his Behaviour in the Examination, shew him to be otherwise. He says, that upon his giving this Account, when he came back to the Inhabitants, Two Men with good Horses went in Pursuit of the said Three Men, who were gone towards *Allegany*, far back beyond the Mountains, and were in hopes of taking them.[5]

---

[5] Peter Heckie and Bryan Conner were arrested and brought to Williamsburg, Virginia, to stand trial. They were both found guilty for the murder of Lifelet Larby on October 21, 1737. The verdict and sentencing were reported in *The Virginia Gazette* issue of October 14-21, 1737:

"These were Two of the Persons who were concern'd [concerned] in the Murder of *Lifelet Larby*, in *Orange* County, of which we formerly gave an Account, as discovered by *William Marr*, another of the Persons concern'd [concerned] in it, who voluntarily came to *Hanover* Court, and confess'd [confessed] the Fact; and being there try'd [tried] by a special Court, was order'd [ordered] to the Public Goal [located in Williamsburg] of this Colony.

"The Confession of the said *Marr* being printed in *this Gazette*, and soon afterwards re-printed in the *Philadelphia* and other *News-Papers*, was the Means of apprehending these Murderers, who fled from the Place where they had committed the Murder, and got into Business in *Pennsylvania*; and tho' [though] they were dispers'd [dispersed] at many Miles Distance from each other, and thought themselves secure, yet there were, by Means of the said Publications, discover'd [discovered], apprehended, and brought together to Justice. The other named *Matthew Conner*, (for there were Four concern'd [concerned]) is not yet taken; but as Murder seldom goes unpunish'd

# The Virginia Gazette, Williamsburg, Virginia, August 12-19, 1737, pg. 1.

*London.*

In Poland the Scarcity of Provisions increase to such a Degree, that great Numbers of the Poor die of Famine in a miserable Manner.[6] This Calamity has sunk the Spirits of the People so low, that at Kaminiech, they imagine they see Spectres and Apparition of the Dead, in the Streets at Night, who kill all Persons they touch or speak to; and some have been so prepossessed with these Reports, that they have actually died with Fear. It is added, that certain Persons having affirmed they saw those Spectres come out of the Tombs in the Church-yards, the Roman-Catholick and Greek Priests had ordered the dead Bodies, that were buried there, be dug up and their Heads cut off, as a Means to prevent their appearing again, which had been executed accordingly.

---

[unpunished], it is not doubted but he will be discover'd [discovered], and meet with his deserv'd [deserved] Fate. On their Tryal, *William Marr* was admitted an Evidence; and the Prisoners at the Bar being conscious of their Guilt, soon confess'd [confessed], viz. *Peter Heckie*, that he shot the said *Larby*; and *Bryan O Conner*, that he was so near at the Time he was kill'd [killed], that he heard him say, *The Lord have Mercy on my Soul*, &c. which, with the Evidence of the said *Marr*, and other material Circumstances corroborating, were convincing to the Jury, who brought them in Guilty." (pg. 3).

Matthew O'Conner was never apprehended for the murder of Lifelet Larby. On November 18, 1737, Peter Heckie and Bryan Conner were hanged at the public gallows on Nicholson Street in Williamsburg, Virginia. Visitors to Colonial Williamsburg have reported hearing a horse drawn carriage and the mummering of a large crowd in the early morning hours before the historic site has opened for the day.

[6] The depletion of supplies brought on by the Russo-Turkish War of 1735-1739 and poor harvests caused famine in Poland and an outbreak of the Bubonic Plague.

## *The Virginia Gazette.* Williamsburg, Virginia, March 21, 1750, pg. 1.

*On Spectres and Apparitions.*

SOME are over-credulous in these Stories, others skeptical and distrustful, and a third Sort perfectly infidel. Mr. Locke[7] assures us, we have as clear an Idea of Spirit, as of Body: But if it be ask'd [asked], How a Spirit, that never was embodied, can form to itself a Body, and come up into a World where it has no Right of Residence, and have all its Organs perfected at once; or how a Spirit, once embodied, but now in a separate State, can take up its Carcass out of the Grave, sufficiently repaired, and make many Resurrections before the last; or how the Dead can counterfeit their own Bodies, and make to themselves an Image of themselves; by what Ways and Means, since Miracles ceas'd [ceased], this Transformation can be effected; by whose Leave and Permission, as by what Power and Authority, or with what wise Design, and for what great Ends and Purposes all this is done, we cannot easily imagine; and the Divine and Philosopher together will find it very difficult to resolve such Questions.

---

[7] John Locke (1632-1704) was an English philosopher and was the most influential of the Enlightenment thinkers of the 18th-century.

Before the Christian Era, some Messages from the other World might be of Use, if not necessary, in some Cases, and on some extraordinary Occasion; but since that Time we want no new, nor can have any surer Information.

### Of Spectres and Apparitions.

SOME are over-credulous in these Stories, others sceptical and distrustful, and a third Sort perfectly infidel. Mr. Locke assures us, we have as clear an Idea of Spirit, as of Body: But if it be ask'd, How a Spirit, that never was embodied, can form to itself a Body, and come up into a World where it has no Right of Residence, and have all its Organs perfected at once; or how a Spirit, once embodied, but now in a separate State, can take up its Carcass out of the Grave, sufficiently repaired, and make many Resurrections before the last; or how the Dead can counterfeit their own Bodies, and make to themselves an Image of themselves; by what Ways and Means, since Miracles ceas'd, this Transformation can be effected; by whose Leave and Permission, or by what Power and Authority, or with what wise Design, and for what great Ends and Purposes all this is done, we cannot easily imagine; and the Divine and Philosopher together will find it very difficult to resolve such Questions.

Before the Christian Æra, some Messages from the other World might be of Use, if not necessary, in some Cases, and on some extraordinary Occasions; but since that Time we want no new, nor can have any surer Informations.

As for the great Evil Spirit, 'tis his Interest to be mask'd or invisible. Among his own sworn Vassals, and upon certain Days of State and Solemnity, he may allow himself to appear in Disguise at a publick Pawwawing (which is attested by a whole Cloud of Travellers) with all the Terrors necessary to confirm his Worshippers in their abject and implicit Slavery: But there is no Instance of his Appearing among us, except what is produc'd by the learned Echard, at a Time when our Country was hardly Christian, and to a Man in such a close Alliance with him, that it was reasonable to suppose, two such dear and intimate Friends should every now and then contrive to have a personal Meeting and Conference.

As for the great Evil Spirit, 'tis his Interest to be mask'd [masked] or invisible. Among his own sworn Vassals, and upon certain Days of State and Solemnity, he may allow himself to appear in Disguise at a publick Pawwawing [powwowing] (which is attested by a whole Cloud of Travelers) with all the Terrors necessary to confirm his Worshippers in their abject and implicit Slavery: But there is no Instance of his Appearing among us, except what is produc'd [produced] by the learned Echard,[8] at a Time when our Country was hardly Christian, and to a Man in such a close Alliance with him, that it was reasonable to suppose, two such dear and intimate Friends should every now and then contrive to have a personal Meeting and Conference.

Some Ghosts and Spectres owe their Existence to a timorous or distempered Imagination, in the Midst of a dark and gloomy Interval; others take their Rise from the reciprocal Pleasure of deluding, and of being deluded: And for the rest, we must impute them to the early Errors of Infancy, and a motley Mixture of the low and vulgar Education: Mothers

---

[8] Jacques Échard (1644-1724) was a French Dominican and historian.

and Grandmothers, Aunts and Nurses, begin the Cheat, and from little Horrors and hideous Stories of Bugbears, Mormoes[9] and Fairies, Raw-head and Bloody Bones,[10] Walking Lights, Will-a Whisps and Hobgoblins, they train us up by Degrees to the Belief of a more substantial Ghost and Apparition. Thus instructed, or thus imposed upon, we begin to listen to the legendary and traditional Accounts of local Ghosts, which, like the Genii of the Ancients, have been reported, Time immemorial, to haunt certain particular Family Seats, and Cities, famous for their Antiquity and Decays. Of this Sort are the Apparitions that are Natives and Denizens of Verulam, Silchester, Reculver, and Rochester; the Demon of Tedworth,[11] the Black Dog of Winchester,[12] and the Barr Guest of York.[13] From hence we proceed to many other Extravagancies of the same Kind, and give some Share of Credit to the out-lying Night Walkers and suburban Ghosts,

---

[9] Archaic term that I was unable to find a definition.

[10] The story of Raw Head and Bloody Bones was a popular English ghost story used to frighten children. The story of Raw Head and Bloody Bones varied depending on the location and time period. In some versions, Bloody Bones is a water demon that hunted children. The legend of Raw Head and Bloody Bones lives on in the United States in the folklore of the Deep South.

[11] The Drummer of Tedworth was a famous case of poltergeist activity that plagued the Mompesson family in Tedworth, Wiltshire, England in the 1660s. The events started after the drum of William Drury was seized by the bailiff and stored at the home of John Mompesson. Drury was accused of vagrancy and was also believed to be a witch. Shortly after the drum was seized it began to be banged by unseen hands at the Mompesson estate.

[12] Spectral black dogs are frequently mentioned in English folklore. In some areas of England, the black dog is an omen of death. There are stories of a black dog seen in the town Twyford, near Winchester, England.

[13] The local ghost of York, England.

rais'd [raised] by petty Printers, and Half-Penny Pamphleteers.

*"The Tedworth Drummer" (1662-1663). (FORTEAN PICTURE LIBRARY)*

The Apparition of Madam Veal,[14] because it recommends the Original Author, Mons. [monsieur] Drelincourt,[15] and his elaborate Discourse upon Death, to all Readers, must therefore be of singular Use to the Translator as well as the Editor: And there are many others, of which no Account can be given but from Trick and Design, to promote some Temporal Interest; as, to bring a hard-mouth'd

---

[14] *A True Relation of the Apparition of One Mrs. Veal* was published anonymously in 1706 and is one of the earliest ghost stories printed in England. Though the story was published anonymously, it has been attributed to the English novelist Daniel Defoe (1660-1731).

[15] Charles Drelincourt (1595-1669) was a French Protestant divine and author of works on theology.

[mouthed] Malefactor to Confession; to oblige an unrelenting Parent to be reconcil'd [reconciled] to a Son or Daughter; or to sink the Rents of a House: And some Houses are said to be haunted just as some old Women are said to be Witches, only because they are squalid and uncouth, dilapidated and out of Repair.

But when we come to read of the Ghost of Sir George Villers,[16] of the Piper of Hammell,[17] the Demon of Moscow, or of the famous German Colonel, mention'd [mentioned] by the Sieur Ponti, and see the great Names of Clarendon, Boyle,[18] &c. affixed to these Accounts, we begin to find Reasons for our Credulity, 'til at last we are convinc'd [convinced] by a whole Conclave of Ghosts, met together in the Works of a Glanvill[19] or a Moreton.

Various Methods are proposed by the Learned for the Laying of Ghosts. Artificial ones are easily quieted, if we only take them for real and substantial Beings, and proceed accordingly. Thus, when a Fryar [friar], personating an Apparition, haunted the Apartment of the late Emperor Joseph;[20] the present King Augustus,[21] then the Imperial Court, flung him out of the Window, and laid him upon the

---

[16] George Villiers, 1st Duke of Buckingham (1592-1628) was the favorite of King James I and his son King Charles I and was murdered by a disgruntled solider at Portsmouth, England. According to legend, the ghost of Sir George Villiers was witnessed before his death by an old servant. The ghost instructed the servant to warn the Duke to stop alienating people or he would not have long to live.

[17] The legend of The Pied Piper of Hamelin dates to the Middle Ages.

[18] Edward Hyde, 1st Earl of Clarendon (1609-1674) was an English statesman and historian.

[19] Joseph Glanvill (1636-1680) was an English writer, philosopher, and clergyman.

[20] John George IV (1668-1694) was the Elector of Saxony from 1691 to his death in 1694.

[21] Augustus II the Strong (1670-1733) was the Elector of Saxony, King of Poland, and Grand Duke of Lithuania.

Pavement so effectually, that he never rose or appear'd [appeared] again.

I shall conclude with a memorable Conference between the late Dr. Fowler, Bishop of Gloucester, and the late Mr. Justice Powell; the former a zealous Defender of Ghosts, and the latter somewhat skeptical about them. They had several Altercations upon the Subject; and once when the Bishop made a Visit to the Justice, the latter contracting the Muscles of his Face into an Air of more than usual Severity, assur'd [assured] the Bishop that since their last Disputation, besides his Lordship's strong Reasons, he had met with no less Proof than ocular Demonstration to convince him of the real Existence of Ghosts. *How!* (says the Bishop) *ocular Demonstration? Well I have preach'd* [preached], *I have printed upon the Subject; but nothing will convince you Scepticks but ocular Demonstrations. I am glad, Mr. Justice, you are become a Convert: But pray, Sir, How went this Affair? I beseech you, let me know the whole Story. My Lord,* (answers the Justice) *as I lay one Night in my Bed, and had gone thro' the better Half of my first Sleep, it being about Twelve; on a sudden I was wak'd* [waked] *by a very strange and uncommon Noise, and heard something coming up Stairs, and stalking directly towards my Room. I had the Courage to rouse myself upon my Pillow, and to draw the Curtain just as I heard my Chamber Door open, and saw a faint glimmering Light enter my Chamber. Of a blue Colour, no doubt,* (says the Bishop). *Of a pale Blue* (answers the Justice). *But give me your Favour, my good Lord! the Light was followed by a tall, meagre, and stern Personage, who seem'd* [seemed] *to be the Age of Seventy, in a long dangling Rug Gown, bound round his Loins with a broad Leathern Girdle: His Beard was thick and grizly; he had a Fur Cap on his Head, and a long Staff in his Hand; his Face was full of Wrinkles, and seem'd* [seemed] *to be a dark and sable Hue. I was struck with the Appearance of so surprising a Figure, and felt some*

*Shocks which I had never before been acquainted with Soon after the Spectre had entered my Room, with a hasty, but somewhat a stately Pace, it drew near my Bed, and star'd* [stared] *me full in the Face. And did you not speak to it?* (interrupted the Bishop, with a good deal of Emotion). *With Submission, my Lord* (says the Justice) *and please to indulge me only in a few Words more. But Mr. Justice! Mr. Justice!* (replies the Bishop still more hastily) *you should have spoken to it: There was Money bid, or Murder committed; and give me Leave to observe, that Murder is a Mater cognizable by Law, and this came regularly into Judgement before you. Well, my Lord, you will have your Way; but in short I did speak it. And what Answer, Mr. Justice, I pray you, What Answer did it make you? My Lord, the Answer was, not without a Thump with the Staff, and a Shake of the Lanthorn* [lantern], *That he was a Watchman of the Night, and came to give me Notice, that he had found the Street Door open; and that unless I rose and shut it, I might chance to be robb'd* [robbed] *before Break of Day.*

The Moment these Words were out of the good Judge's Mouth, the Bishop vanish'd [vanished] with much more Haste than did the suppos'd [supposed] Ghost, and in as great a Surprize at the Justice's Scepticism, as the Justice was in at the Bishop's Credulity.

## *The South-Carolina and American General Gazette,*
## Charleston, South Carolina, July 18, 1770, pg. 3.

THE COMPLETE WIZZARD; Being a Collection of authentick and entertaining Narratives of the real Existence and Appearance of Ghosts, Demons, and Spectres: Together with several wonderful Instances of the Effects of Witchcraft.

To which is prefixed, an Account of haunted Houses, and subjoined, a Treatise on the Effects of Magick. *Price* 2s. 6d.

THE

*CONNECTICUT*

*COURANT*

*Containing the freshest and most important* *advices, both Foreign and Domestic*

## *Hartford Courant,* Hartford, Connecticut, January 29-February 5, 1771, pg. 3.

*These may certify all* whom it may concern That whereas there has been a report spread abroad, that Joseph Bidwell[22] of Glastonbury, did in the month of May, in the year A. D. 1769 by whipping, or some other way, make way with David Brewer a servant boy to said Bidwell, (a lad of about 14 or 15 years of age) and said boy has not been seen nor heard of since. And that said Brewers apparition has appeared to Charles Riley,[23] and told him his body was under the floor, and the said Riley on the 28th day of January, A. D. 1771, apply'd [applied] to us the subscribers, justices of the peace for Hartford county; that he had seen Brewers apparition on the friday before at noon day, within about twenty rods of said Bidwell's barn. We knowing said Riley to be a man not depended upon but to satisfy people abroad, we went on said 28th day, with about twenty judicious men, and pulled up said

---

[22] Joseph Bidwell (1726-1796) lived in Glastonbury, Connecticut, and is buried in Old South Cemetery.

[23] Charles Riley (unknown-1797) was a neighbor of Joseph Bidwell and his name appears on the muster roll of the 7th Connecticut Regiment during the Revolutionary War.

Bidwell's barn floor, and dug in several places, and found no appearance of any breakage of earth, until we were all satisfied there was no person there, and there has five persons of lawful age, testified under oath, that they have seen said David Brewer since he run away from said Bidwell.

JONATHAN HALE,[24] Justice Peace.

WILLIAM WELLS,[25] Justice Peace.

Glastonbury, Feb. 2, 1771.

## *The Pennsylvania Packet,* Philadelphia, Pennsylvania, August 22, 1785, pg. 3.

THE FRIGHTFUL GHOST.

    All the *old women* in the city, as well *males* as *females* (for let the philosphers argue as they will, there are centainly *male old women*; i.e. those males who delight in the marvellous— the prodigious—the supernatural—who regulate their actions, by omens, and lucky or unlucky dreams—who believe as "strong as proof of holy writ,"[26] in witches, warlocks, dreadful ghosts and apparitions) are highly regaled by the following *amazing story* of a vengeful sprite. (But it is to be observed, that it is only collected from common fame, and that we do not vouch for the truth of any part of it).

---

[24] Captain Jonathan Hale (1696-1772) was a respected member of the Glastonbury and is buried in Green Cemetery.
[25] William Wells (1724-1778) like his neighbors, he lived his entire life in Glastonbury and is buried in Green Cemetery.
[26] "Trifles light as air/Are to the jealous confirmations strong/As proofs of holy writ" (Act III, Scene 4) from *Othello* by William Shakespeare (1603).

In the hold of a vessel now in our river, there was lately found a human skeleton, from which the flesh had all rotted away: it was interred in the Potter's field, without holding any inquest. The ghost to whom it belonged, taking this neglect in high dudgeon, comes to the vessel, and with knockings, scrapings & scratchings—white sheets, pallied countenance and a bloody knife—and all the other apparatus befitting a ghost of consequence, pays regular visits to the tars, praying them to have justice done to his manes [remains], by bringing the murderer to condign punishment. The person accused is the mate of a vessel which is, by the ghost's account, to arrive speedily in this port. So superstitious were the sailors, that they applied to judge M'Kean[27] to take their examinations on the charge of the ghost.—This, we hear, the judge refused— But they applied to some other magistrate, who received their depositions, and the mate is hourly looked for.—A *most important wager* is laid on this business—An old man staked his *tobacco-pouch* against an *old gossop's* [gossip's] *snuff-box*, that the ghost will, on being thrice called by court, ascend through the floor, *in propria persona*,[28] with the marks of the wounds quite tangible—This, the old man adds, has *quite the mode* with all *genuine ghosts* who have appeared since the days of the *witch of Endor*.[29]

---

[27] Thomas McKean (1734-1817) was a lawyer and politician. McKean was a signer of the Declaration of Independence and the Articles of Confederation. From 1777 to 1799, McKean served as the Chief Justice of Pennsylvania.

[28] Latin for "in his or her own person."

[29] The Witch of Endor appears in the Old Testament in the Book of 1 Samuel 28: 3-25. Despite banning conjuring of spirits, King Saul of Israel visited the Witch of Endor to communicate with the spirit of the prophet Samuel. Saul was concerned about the fate of his army in an upcoming battle against the Philistines. The spirit of Samuel warned Saul that the king and his three sons would die in the battle. Samuel's prediction proved to be correct.

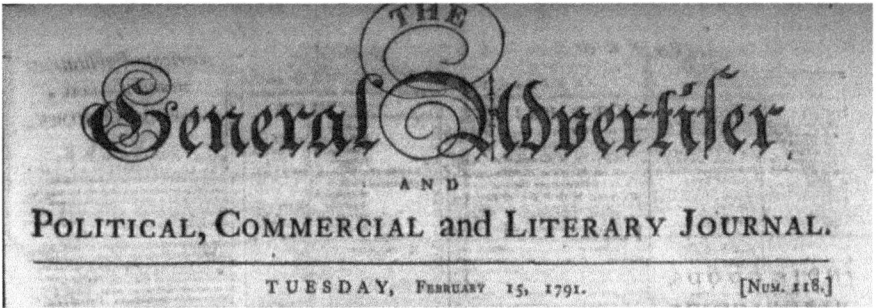

## Aurora General Advertiser, Philadelphia, Pennsylvania, February 15, 1791, pg. 2.

*From a late Irish Newspaper.*

THE GHOST OF SPENDLIN'S CASTLE.

ON the banks of the river Annan stands Spendlin [Spedlins] Castle,[30] which has long been, as it is at present, the property of an ancient and respectable family, the Jardins of Applegarth.   Its form, like most of those buildings, is a strange, square, vaulted tower, with walls of a great thickness, flanked by round turrets, at the angles.

But this building is chiefly famous for being haunted by a bogle or ghost; the story of which is related so

---

[30] Spedlins Tower is located three miles north of Lochmaben, Scotland, and was the ancestral home of the Jardins of Applegarth from the 12th to the 19th-century.  The tower was constructed in 1605 and is still used as a residence.

seriously by an honest old woman who lives on the spot, that there is no doubt she believes every syllable of it.

*Spedlins Tower (Grose, 1789)*

In the time of the late Sir John's grandfather,[31] a person named Porteus,[32] living in the parish of Applegarth, was taken up on suspicion of setting fire to a mill, and confined in the late Lord's prison, the pit, or dungeons at the castle. The Lord being suddenly called to Edinburgh on some pressing and unexpected business, in his hurry forgot to leave the key of the pit, which he always held in his own custody. Before he discovered his mistake, and could send back the key, which he did the moment he found it out, the man was starved to death, having first, through the extremity of hunger, gnawed off one of his hands.—Ever after that time the Castle was terribly haunted, till a chaplain of the family

---

[31] This is a reference to Alexander Jardine of Applegirth (c. 1599-c. 1629) and his grandson Sir John Jardine of Applegirth, 3rd Baronet (1683-1737).

[32] James "Dunty" Porteous was the miller for the Village of Milhousebridge and delivered bread to Spedlins Tower. Porteous was known in the community for his quarrelsome temper. This earned him the nickname "Dunty," the Old English term for argument.

exorcised and confined the bogle to the pit, whence it could never come out, so long as a bible which he had used on that business, remained in the castle. It is said that the chaplain did not long survive the operation. The ghost, however, kept quietly within the bounds of his prison till a long time after, when the bible, which was used by the whole family, required a new binding, for which purpose it was sent to Edinburgh. The ghost, taking advantage of its absence, was extremely boisterous in the pit, seeming as if it would break through the iron door, and making a noise like that of a large bird fluttering its wings. The bible being returned, and the pit filled up, every thing has since remained perfectly quiet. But the good woman declares, that should it again be taken off the premises, no consideration whatsoever would induce her to remain there a single night.[33]

## *The Vermont Gazette,* Bennington, Vermont, June 15, 1792, pg. 4.

A GHOST.

A GIRL who was [a] servant in a house reputed to be haunted, was suspected and at length fairly convicted of pregnancy; she fell on her knees before her mistress, and craved forgiveness, alleging indeed that she ought not be blamed, for it was entirely the ghost's fault. "The ghost's fault!" exclaimed the mistress, "how could that possibly happen?" "Why indeed madam!" replied the simple girl, "the

---

[33] The ghost of Porteous continued to haunt the Jardine family. According to legend, it was Porteous's ghost which caused the family to flee Spedlins Tower to Jardine Hall across the River Annan. Porteous still haunts Spedlins Tower, but he has mellowed over time. It is said that if visitors put a stick in the dungeon window it will come out chewed on by Porteous.

ghost one dark night made a huge noise, and almost terrified me out of my seven senses. I told JOHN how it had *sarved* [scared] me, and he persuaded me how spirits never appeared, when *two people* slept together. So as I liked his company better than the ghosteses, and was mortally afraid of ghostesses, I went along with him, and so, indeed and indeed madam I should never have lost my *vartue* [virtue], if it had not been for fear of the ghosteses."

## *The Philadelphia Inquirer.* Philadelphia, Pennsylvania, January 19, 1798, pg. 3.

NEW-YORK, JAN. 10.
*New-Goal, (in the Fields) Jan.* 10, 1798

A true and surprising account of the apparition or ghost of a woman, that has appeared several nights past and in the New-Goal [jail], to the great terror and affright of the prisoners, many of whom are ready to confirm the truth of it on oath.

Capt. Fish declares that for several nights past, the apparition of a woman has haunted the goal from room to room, this and the last week, followed and encircled by a radiant light, dressed in a white flowing robe and a turban on her head, seemingly of a pleading but dejected countenance. Capt. Fish declares that about twelve o'clock on Friday night this apparition came to his bedside, and drew the curtains, looking steadfastly at him for some time, which so affrighted him, that he adjured her in the name of the Father, Son, and Holy Ghost, to tell him who she was, or why she came in "so questionable a shape," when she casting a look of sorrow, accompanied with most ineffable sweetness gradually disappeared in the sight of several other prisoners who were in the room, and are ready to testify the truth of what is here advanced.

Mr. Miller another debtor[34] in the same room, going to the upper hall, about one in the morning, was met by the same woman who pulled him by the coat, which so alarmed and frightened him that he stood petrified as a statue; when he came a little to himself he saw her gradually advance to the window, from which she vanished. He then called to the watchman to ask him if he had seen it, he declared he did, and that he had seen it vanish from the same window several nights successively.

Mr. Miller further declares, that after she was gone, a large globe of fire of the most beautiful and diversified colours rolled up and down the hall for the space of five minutes; and then of a sudden burst with a dreadful explosion, which left him in total darkness, which still affrighted him worse than the first rencountre of the apparition; when making but one step from the top of the stairs to the bottom, he recovered his room, in a condition of understandable terror.

---

[34] In this period a person could be imprisoned for an unpaid debt.

The Friday following Mr. Evans, being asleep in his bed, was suddenly awakened by something drawing open the curtains of his bed, when he perceived the figure of a beautiful woman, arrayed in white, looking steadfastly on him, which much alarmed him; he communicated his fear to another man who was in the same bed with him, who also saw it with terror and astonishment. It continued a considerable time by the bedside in a contemplative posture, often putting her hand on the left side of her robe, which seemed to be tinged with blood, and then heaving a deep sigh, vanished through the wall.

Mr. Hewit a few evenings after this, in the dead of the night being alarmed in his sleep, suddenly leaped out of bed, and the first thing presented to his view was the apparition of this woman, who with the most placid countenance seemed to claim his pity; but frightened to the greatest degree at so uncommon an appearance, and fear closing his power of utterance, he leaped again into bed, covering himself over head and ears, with every particle of the bed furniture that was within his grasp. In a few minutes after, this apparition disappeared, which was accompanied by a solemn, hollow rumbling noise, leaving him "The utmost exacerbation of human terror."

The prisoners in general further declare, that almost every night about twelve o'clock there appears a large ball of fire at intervals, which illuminates every room in the goal for a time.

*The Philadelphia Inquirer.* Philadelphia, Pennsylvania, February 7, 1798, pg. 2.

THE GHOST.

An account of a remarkable effort to recover liberty, and which may be depended on as a fact.

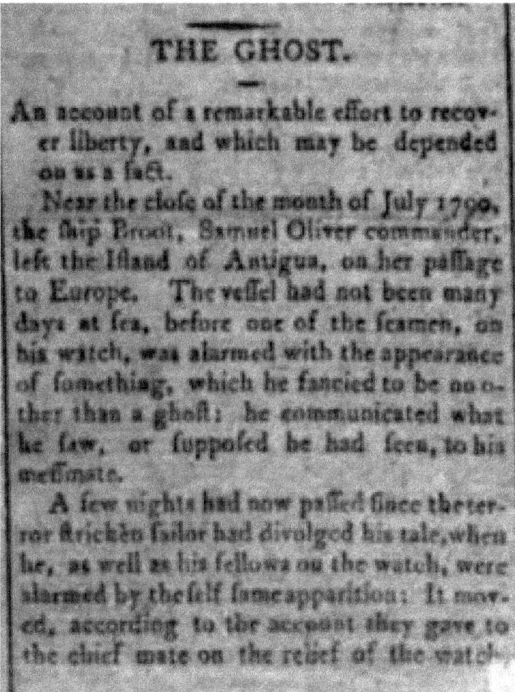

Near the close of the month July 1790, the ship Broot, Samuel Oliver commander, left the Island of Antigua, on her passage to Europe. The vessel had not been many days at sea, before one of the seamen, on his watch, was alarmed with the appearance of something, which he fancied to be no other than a ghost; he communicated what he saw, or supposed he had seen, to his messmates.

A few nights had now passed since the terror stricken sailor had divulged his tale, when he, as well as his fellows on watch, were alarmed by the selfsame apparition: It moved, according to the account they gave to the chief mate on the relief of the watch in slow pace all round the forecastle;[35] and after continuing sometime there vanished behind the windlass.[36]  The mate affected to laugh at the account; nevertheless he had his fears; and it was agreed on that himself together with the boatswain[37] and several other stout hearted fellows, should assist the watch to discover, if possible, what it was which had so much alarmed the greatest part of the crew.  The main deck was accordingly walked by these heroes, night after night, without the ghost making its appearance.  Having been upwards of twenty days at sea, the weather in the night became boisterous; the winds blew; the thunder rolled awfully, and the lightning flashed terrifically vivid; all hands were called up to assist the ship by their labors; and in the midst of their professional employ the ghost again made its appearance; and it was now seen by the whole crew (the captain excepted): One of those employed on the quarter deck[38] rushed forwards towards the supposed phantom; and at the instant it seemed within his grasp, a flash of lightening of the most tremendous sort covered it from his sight: This was seen by the men on the yards, who were reefing[39] the several sails, and who, one and all, declared it could be no other than the devil, as he sunk from the attempt of the sailor in a flash of fire.  Several of the sailors were positive it could be no other than the evil spirit, for reasons to them the most sufficient; that they missed their beef, their biscuit and their grog, whenever all hands were called on deck; that they has also heard that ghosts could neither eat

---

[35] The upper deck of a sailing ship.

[36] A windlass is the mechanization that is used to let-out and heave-up an anchor.

[37] The boatswain is an officer in charge of the ship's crew.

[38] The quarterdeck is part of the upper deck abaft the mainmast. This section is typically reserved only for the ship's officers, guests, and passengers.

[39] Reducing the area of the sails.

nor drink; and what confirmed them stronger in their belief of it being no other than lucifer himself was, from its vanishing the preceding night, in a flame of fire; and some of them were not wanting to give it as their opinion, that he had raised the storm.

The affair of the ghost had now become serious, and the mate accordingly determined on acquainting the captain with the whole business on the following day: This being accordingly done, the captain heard the relation with some surprise, and communicated the mysterious account to his passengers, asking them at the same time their advice. It was agreed upon to walk the deck that night, and there form their opinion of the truth of the report: They began their march about ten, and continued it until the break of day; the ghost or devil did not appear; and bringing to mind what was said by some of our greatest poets, that the troubled spirits haunt our region but while darkness and obscurity fill the void, they retired to their beds, probably well satisfied with the event of their watch. The captain and passengers now put down the whole story as no other than the effect of imagination in the crew: But the men were not to be thus amused out of the opinion which they all firmly believed; and they still persisted in what they had said and seen: what served to heighten their credulity still more, was an event which had taken place but a few hours before; [unclear]. This excited new curiosity; and the captain, finding it would be difficult to prevail over their prejudices, offered a reward to him or them who would discover who or what this devil was. A fellow who had, through the whole of this singular affair, appeared less alarmed than the rest, was the first to undertake the business; and of the ship's company readily agreed to assist in the discovery. To work they went, when, after having moved upwards of forty hogshead of sugar, the spirit was discovered asleep in an empty water butt: It was no other than a Negro man of about twenty years of age, who, with a view of recovering his liberty, had there secreted himself. His story, when brought into the cabin, was nearly as follows: That he belonged to a Mr. Alexander Coates,[40] ship builder in the town of St. John's; that his master having sent him in a canoe to get turtle grass, and put it on board this vessel, he accordingly did so, and it being the dusk of the evening when he delivered it, a tho't [thought] struck him, that such an opportunity would probably never offer again for his getting to England,[41] he therefore slipped down a rope which was hanging over the stern, put his jacket into a canoe, and keeping hold of the stern rope, cut his boat adrift, and ascended the vessel undiscovered. He now crept into the fore hatchway, and got into the hold, where, finding the empty watercask, he took out its head, and therein he secreted himself during the space of thirty three days, seven of which was while the ship lay in St. John's harbor (during which time the canoe had been picked up, and the man was given up as drowned), and twenty-six at sea. His manner of living was, when the sailors were all on deck, he would steal out, and pick up what he could find, and carry it to his tub; and also turnout at night when he thought all quiet, to breathe refreshing air. After the discovery he worked as a seaman, having, previous to this trip made two voyages to Liverpool; and he was named by the sailors Jack Ghost; and those brave fellows seemed

---

[40] Alexander Coates (1734-1807) was a merchant and sugar planter on the British colony of Antigua. Slavery was abolished in the British colonies in 1834.

[41] In 1772, William Murray, 1st Earl of Mansfield, Chief Justice of the King's Bench, ruled in the case *Somerset v Stewart* that slavery was unsupported by common law in England and Wales. The ruling did not apply to Britain's colonies. The ruling in the Somerset case inspired countless slaves to flee to England.

rather diverted than hurt by the consternation he had thrown them into.

(*N. Y. paper*)

## *Federal Galaxy,* Brattleboro, Vermont, 13 March 1798, pg. 4.

BEAUTIFUL GHOST!
LITCHFIELD, Jan. 31.

UNDER the N. York head of the 10ᵗʰ inst. is published, "A true and surprising account of the apparition or ghost of a woman, that has appeared several nights past in the Goal (in the fields) to the great terror and affright of the prisoners—many of whom are ready to confirm the truth of it on oath." The story is well told; and to give it the appearance of truth, the names of several reputable prisoners (debtors) are introduced; who described the ghost as dressed in a white flowing robe, tinged with blood on the left side, and a turban on her head; of a pleading placid countenance, but much dejected—followed and encircled by a radiant light, and sometimes preceded by a globe of fire. The recital is frightful in the extreme—calculated to make

*"Thy knotted and combined locks to part,*
*And each particular hair to stand on end,*
*Like quills upon the fretful Porcupine."*[42]

*I wonder what it means?* has been vociferated by a thousand tongues; the fact is, a young married woman, whose husband was confined for debt, despairing of means (the creditor being uncharitable and stubborn) conjured up the ghost; and trusting the secret with a confidential printer; the

---

[42] Line from William Shakespeare's play *Hamlet* (Act 1, Scene 5. 1).

account was printed before it was lisped abroad, and immediately put into the hawkers hands for sale: The project succeeded — business was suspended: The multitude flocked about the goal. And here again the hawkers were at their posts, vending their bills of the appearance and performances of the ghost. The debtor's wife having in a short time, raised a sufficient sum to satisfy his creditors, and to gladden his heart with a nourishing repay — *Miss Puss was let out of the bag*, and the abashed multitude returned, one to his stall and the other to his merchandise.

# Chapter II

## Witches

The belief in witchcraft dates to the ancient world. In pre-Christian times, witches or cunning folk were trusted members of the community who were consulted for their medical knowledge. The reliance on cunning folk changed with the spread of the Catholic Church which labeled witches as the agents of the devil. Fear of witchcraft continued in England after the Protestant Reformation, particularly during the reign of King James VI and I (1566-1625). James was obsessed with the perceived threat of witches to the peace and stability of his kingdom and published a treatise on witchcraft *Daemonologie* in 1597.

In *Daemonologie*, James advocated for a series of tests to determine if a person was a witch. One of the most popular tests used was a trial by water, otherwise known as ducking. This test required a person to be ducked in water. The suspected witch would be stripped naked to ensure that he or she did not have any charms or pins on their person that would help them past the test. The unfortunate person was then had their hands and feet bound, sometimes they were even tied in a sheet or a bag, then dumped in a lake or pond. If the person was a witch, the accused would float because by consorted with the devil they had rejected their baptism. If the person was innocent of the accusation of witchcraft, they would sink to the bottom of the pond. The person would then be pulled out of the water so that they would not drown.

The most notorious witch trials that took place in England and the American colonies occurred in 17th-century. The Pendle Hill Witch Trials of 1612 in Lancashire, England resulted in the executions of ten men and women and the Salem Witch Trials of 1692 in the Massachusetts Bay Colony resulted in the executions of nineteen men and women came to symbolize the excess of the eras witch hunts.

While Pendle Hill and Salem stand out for the high number of victims, witch trials continued in England and America until the mid-1700s. In Virginia, Grace Sherwood was ducked in 1706 after allegations of witchcraft by jealous neighbors. As discussed in the introduction, the Witchcraft Act of 1735 made it illegal for a person to be accused of witchcraft. Though witch trials were abolished, the persecution of suspected witches continued as the following accounts document.

*A trial by water also known as ducking.*

Numb. CI.

# THE
# Pennſylvania *GAZETTE.*

*Containing the freſheſt Advices Foreign and Domeſtick.*

From Thurſday, October 15. to Thurſday, October 22. 1730.

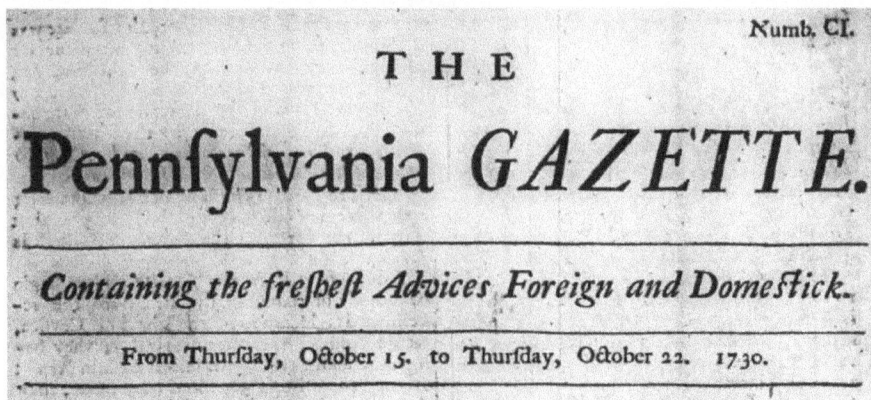

## *The Pennsylvania Gazette,* Philadelphia, Pennsylvania, October 15-22, 1730, pg. 3-4.[43]

BURLINGTON, Oct. 12. Saturday last at *Mount-Holly*, about 8 Miles from this Place, near 300 People were gathered together to see an Experiment or two tried on some Persons accused of Witchcraft. It seems the Accused had been charged with making their Neighbours Sheep dance in an uncommon Manner, and with causing Hogs to speak, and sing Psalms, &c. to the great Terror and Amazement of the King's[44] good and peaceable Subjects in this Province; and the Accusers being very positive that if the Accused were weighed in Scales against a Bible, the Bible would prove too heavy for them; or that, if they were bound and put into the River, they would swim; the said Accused desirous to make their Innocence appear, voluntarily offered to undergo the

---

[43] This piece was written by Benjamin Franklin as a satire. The events described never happened, instead it was Franklin's way to satirize those who relied on superstition and ignorance over rational thinking. Franklin's audience would have recognized the piece as a parody. Benjamin Franklin was the publisher of *The Pennsylvania Gazette* from 1729 till his retirement in 1748.

[44] King George II of Great Britain (1683-1760) reigned from 1727 to 1760.

*BURLINGTON, Oct. 12.* Saturday laſt at *Mount-Holly*, about 8 Miles from this Place, near 300 People were gathered together to ſee an Experiment or two tried on ſome Perſons accuſed of Witchcraft. It ſeems the Accuſed had been charged with making their Neighbours Sheep dance in an uncommon Manner, and with cauſing Hogs to ſpeak, and ſing Pſalms, &c. to the great Terror and Amazement of the King's good and peaceable Subjects in this Province; and the Accuſers being very poſitive that if the Accuſed were weighed in Scales againſt a Bible, the Bible would prove too heavy for them; or that, if they were bound and put into the River, they would ſwim; the ſaid Accuſed deſirous to make their Innocence appear, voluntarily offered to undergo the ſaid Trials, if 2 of the moſt violent of their Accuſers would be tried with them. Accordingly the Time and Place was agreed on, and advertiſed about the Country; The Accuſers were 1 Man and 1 Woman; and the Accuſed the ſame. The Parties being met, and the People got together, a grand Conſultation was held, before they proceeded to Trial; in which it was agreed to uſe the Scales firſt; and a Committe of Men were appointed to ſearch the Men, and a Committee of Women to ſearch the Women, to ſee if they had any Thing of Weight about them, particularly Pins. After the Scrutiny was over, a huge great Bible belonging to the Juſtice of the Place was provided, and a Lane through the Populace was made from the Juſtices Houſe to the Scales, which were fixed on a Gallows erected for that Purpoſe oppoſite to the Houſe, that the Juſtice's Wife

said Trials, if 2 of the most violent of their Accusers would be tried with them. Accordingly the Times and Place was agreed on, and advertised about the Country; The Accusers were 1 Man and 1 Woman; and the Accused the same. The Parties being met, and the People got together, a grand Consultation was held, before they proceeded to Trial; in which it was agreed to use the Scales first; and a Committee of Men were appointed to search the Men, and a Committee of Women to search the Women, to see if they had any Thing of Weight about them, particularly Pins. After the Scrutiny was over, a huge great Bible belonging to the Justice of the Place was provided, and a Lane through the Populace was made from the Justices House to the Scales, which were fixed on a Gallows erected for that Purpose opposite to the House, that the Justice's Wife and the rest of the Ladies might see the Trial, without coming amongst the Mob; and after the Manner of *Moorsfield*, a large Ring was also made. Then came out of the House a grave tall Man carrying the Holy Writ before the supposed Wizard, &c. (as solemnly as the Sword-bearer of *London* before the Lord Mayor) the Wizard was first put in the Scale, and over him was read a Chapter out of the Books of *Moses*,[45] and then the Bible was put in the other Scale, (which being kept down before) was immediately let go; but to the great Surprise of the Spectators, Flesh and Bones came down plump, and outweighed that great good Book by abundance. After the same Manner, the others were served, and their Lumps of Mortality severally were too heavy for *Moses* and all the Prophets and Apostles. This being over, the Accusers and the rest of the Mob, not satisfied with this Experiment, would have the Trial by Water; accordingly a most solemn Procession was made to the Mill-pond; where both Accused and Accusers being stripp'd [stripped] (having only to the Women [in] their Shifts) were bound Hand and Foot, and severally placed in the Water, lengthways, from the Side of a Barge or Flat [boat], having for Security only a Rope about the Middle of each, which was held by some in the Flat [boat]. The Accuser Man being thin and spare, with some Difficulty began to sink at last; but the rest every one of them swam very light upon the Water. A Sailor in the Flat [boat] jump'd [jumped] out upon the Back of the Man accused, thinking to drive him down to the Bottom; but the Person bound, without any Help, came up some time before the other. The Woman Accuser, being told that she did not sink, would be duck'd [ducked] a second Time; when she swam again as light as before. Upon which she declared, That she believed the Accused had bewitched her to make her so light, and that she would be duck'd [ducked] again a Hundred Times, but she would duck the Devil out of her. The

---

[45] The books of Moses are: Genesis, Exodus, Leviticus, Numbers, and Deuteronomy.

accused Man, being surpriz'd [surprised] at his own Swimming, and not so confident of his Innocence as before, but said, *If I am a Witch, it is more than I know.* The more thinking Part of the Spectators were of Opinion, that any Person so bound and plac'd [placed] in the Water (unless they were mere Skin and Bones) would swim till their Breath was gone, and their Lungs fill'd [filled] with Water. But it being the general Belief of the Populace, that the Womens Shifts, and the Garters with which they were bound hel'd [helped] to support them; it is said they are to be tried again the next warm Weather, naked.

*A witch dunking at a millpond in Norfolk, England in the 17th-century*

## *The Pennsylvania Gazette,* Philadelphia, Pennsylvania, April 15-22, 1731, pg. 2.

*Jan.* 20.

We are told from Frome, in Somersetshire, that a poor old Woman was lately seized by the Populace, near that Town, on a Pretence that she was a Witch, and had bewitched one Man's Child, and another Man's Cow; they dragged the poor Creature so long through a Mill-pond, that she expired in an Hour after; for which vile Action, 3 of the Chief of them are committed to Prison, and 'tis hop'd [hoped] they will be punished according to their Demerits.

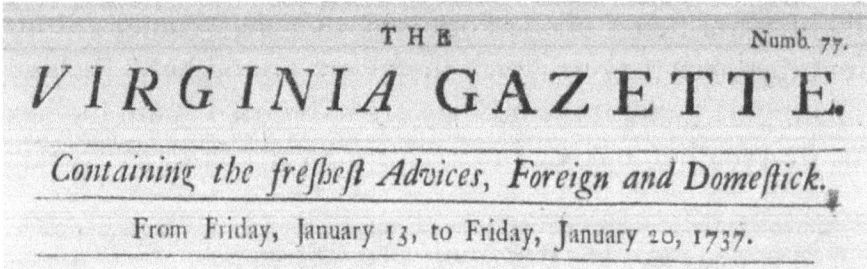

THE

*VIRGINIA* GAZETTE.

*Containing the freſheſt Advices, Foreign and Domeſtick.*

From Friday, January 13, to Friday, January 20, 1737.

## *The Virginia Gazette,* Williamsburg, Virginia, January 13-20, 1737, pg. 1.

*From the* Whitehall Evening-Post
*London, July* 21, 1736.

SIR,

I Send you enclos'd [enclosed] a very remarkable Letter concerning the late cruel Usage of a poor old Woman in Bedfordshire, who was suspect'd [suspected] of being a Witch. You will see by it, that the late Law for Abolishing the Act against Witches, has not abolish'd [abolished] the Credulity of the Country People;[46] but I hope it has made proper Provision for punishing their Barbarity on such Occasion.

---

[46] The Witchcraft Act of 1735 made it a crime to accuse a person of being a witch or practicing magic. This abolished the hunting and punishment of witches by legal authorities.

I am, SIR.

Yours, &c. A. B.


*Extract of a Letter about the Tryal of a* WITCH.

*Oakley.* Three Miles from *Bedford.*


*SIR,*

THE People here are so prejudic'd [prejudiced] in the Belief of *Witches*, that you would think your self in *Lapland*,[47] was you to hear their ridiculous Stories. There is not a Village in the Neighbourhood but has Two or Three. About a Week ago I was pre'ent [present] at the Ceremony of Ducking a Witch; a particular Account of which, may not perhaps be disagreeable to you.

An Old Woman of about 60 Years of Age, had long lain under an Imputation of Witchcraft; who, being willing (for her own Sake and her Children's) to clear her self, consented to be duck'd [ducked]; and the Parish Office promis'd [promised] her a Guinea, if she should sink: The Place appointed for the Operation, was in the River *Oust*, by a Mill; there were, I believe, 500 Spectators: About 11 o'Clock in the Forenoon, the Woman came, and was tied up in a wet Sheet, all but her Face and Hands; her Toes were tied close together, as were also her Thumbs, and her Hands tied to the small of her Legs: They fasten'd [fastened] a Rope about her Middle, and the pull'd [pulled] off her Cap in search for Pins, for their Notion is, if they have but one Pin about 'em, they won't sink.

---

[47] This is a reference to Lapland, Sweden. Lapland was home during the 16th to 17th centuries to the Sámi people, called the Lapps, in English. The Sámi people had strong shamanistic traditions and practiced magic. Despite the prevalence for witch trials in Europe between the 16th to 18th centuries, there were few witch trials in Lapland.

When all Preliminaries were settled, she was thrown in: but, unhappily for the poor Creature, she floated; tho' her Head was all the while under Water: Upon this there was a confuse'd [confused] Cry, *A Witch! a Witch! Hang her! Drown her!* She was in the Water about one Minute and a Half, and was then taken out half drown'd [drowned]; when she had recovered Breath, the Experiment was repeated twice more, but with the same Success; for she floated each Time; which was a plain Demonstration of Guilt to the ignorant Multitude: For notwithstanding the poor Creature was laid upon the Grass, speechless, and almost dead, they were so far from shewing [showing] her any Pity or Compassion, that they strove who should be the most forward in loading her with Reproaches. Such is the dire Effect of popular Prejudice! As for my Part, I stood against the Torrent, and when I had cut the Strings which tied her, had her carried back to the Mill, and endeavored to convince the People of the Uncertainty of the Experiment, and offer'd [offered] to lay Five to One, that any Woman of her Age, so tied up in a loose Sheet, would float; but all to no Purpose, for I was very near being mobb'd [mobbed]. Some Time after, the Woman came out; and one of the Company happe'd [happened] to mention another Experiment to try a Witch, which was to weigh her against the *Church Bible*; for a Witch it seems, could not outweigh it. I immediately seconded that Motion (as thinking it might be of Service to the poor Woman) and made use of an Argument, which (tho' as weak as *King *James's*,[48] for their not sinking) had some Weight with the People; for I told them, if she was a Witch, she certainly dealt with the Devil; and the Bible was undoubtedly the *Word of God*, it must weigh more than all the

---

[48] King James VI and I (1566-1625) was King of Scotland from 1567 and King of England from 1603 until 1625. James was concerned about witchcraft and in 1597 wrote *Daemonologie* his treatise on the subject.

DÆMONOLOGIE,
IN FORME
OF A DIA-
LOGVE,

*Diuided into three books:*

WRITTEN BY THE HIGH
and mightie Prince, I AME S by the
*grace of God King of* England,
Scotland, France *and* Ireland,
*Defender of the Faith, &c.*

LONDON,
Printed by *Arnold Hatfield* for
*Robert VVald-graue.*
1 6 0 3

Title page of *Daemonologie* written by King James I.

*Works of the Devil.* This seem'd [seemed] reasonable to several;
and those that did not think it so, could not answer it: At last,
the Question was carried, and she was weighed against the
Bible; which weighing about twelve Pounds, she outweighed

it. This convinc'd [convinced] some, and stagger'd [staggered] others; but some who believ'd [believed] thro' thick and thin, went away fully assured, that she was a Witch, and endeavoured to inculcate that Belief into all others.
I am, SIR,
Your very humble Servant.

*King James's *Argument why* Witches *would not sink, was this*; They had renounced their *Baptism by Water*, and therefore the *Water* would not receive them.


## *The Pennsylvania Gazette.* Philadelphia, Pennsylvania, April 13-20, 1738, pg. 2.

BRISTOL, *Jan.* 7. From Porishead [Portishead] we have a very odd Account of an Affair which passed there for Witchcraft: One Flower, an old Taylor [tailor], noted for nursing Parish Children for 18 *d.* [pence] per Week, and his Wife, have severely felt the Effects of it; for at every instant either one or the other had a Bang on the Head, or some other part of the Body, with large Stones, Spoons, Knives, &c. and divers People who witnessed the House out of Curiosity, met with the same Treatment, and saw the Windows broke, but knew not by the what Means; and such was the Fear of many, that they thought it dangerous to enter the House. At length a Gentlewoman of this City, who happen'd [happened] to be at a Gentleman's Seat near that Place, hearing of this reported by the Family where she resided, and putting no Faith in such Stories, resolved, like the rest, to visit the bewitched House, and saw several Things flung about, but imperceivable from whence; and repeating her Visit at length began to look with a suspicious Eye on a little Girl of about 12 Years old, Grand-

Daughter to the old People, who she always perceiv'd [perceived] placed herself in a Window behind whatever Persons came into the Room, and she receiving a Blow on the Arm with a Spoon, conjectured it must come from the Girl, and therefore immediately search'd [searched] her, and to her Surprize found two Pockets full of large Pebble-Stones, &c. under her Petticoats, which she artfully flung at convenient Opportunities, and carry'd [carried] this Subtility so far, as to occasion much Wonder that a little Witch so young could manage her Scheme so well to deceive a whole Parish; for besides this, she had a Knack in changing her Voice to several Tones. The Gentlewoman had the Thanks of the whole Parish for discovering this young Witch.

## *The Virginia Gazette,* Williamsburg, Virginia, May 4-11, 1739, pg. 2.

*Feversham, Dec.* 25. A barbarous Murder was lately committed on Jane Plane, by Stephan Diaper, one of the most stupid Villains that ever was formed with human Shape; of which the Story is as follows, viz. Mr. James Bunce, of Ospringe near Feversham, gives every St. Thomas's Day,[49] a certain Measure of Wheat to every poor Woman that comes and asks for the same; amongst the Number was Jane Plane, a poor Widow Woman of an unblemished Character, aged between Sixty and Seventy Years, who was ordered by Mr. Bunce to have the Measure. The Villain, who was ordered to measure the Corn, took it into his Head, that this poor

---

[49] St. Thomas's Day was celebrated in England on December 21 as part of the Christmas season. On St. Thomas's Day, wealthy households would distribute grain to the poor, who then used the grain to make their Christmas dinner.

Creature was a Witch, and bethought himself a Stratagem, which he had heard, to know them by; this was, that no Witch had Power to receive more than Measure, which proved the Death of the innocent Creature; for her Modesty was so great, that she told him, at seeing Heap-measure, his Master did not allow of it, neither did she desire any more than he was willing to give; this, and this only, urged on her Fate; for she no sooner refus'd [refused], but he drew his Knife, and stabbed her in above Forty Places. Mr. Bunce was in the Room at the same Time, with a Child in his Arms, and two others by his Side; not knowing where the Villain would stop, his first Care was to secure the Children; then calling in three other of his Servants, went and seized the Ruffian, who gloried in his Action.

## *Virginia Gazette,* Williamsburg, Virginia, July 18, 1751, pg. 2-3.

*April* 24.    Last Monday the following most extraordinary Affair happened at Tring in Hertfordshire; some of the Country People having entertained an Opinion that an Old Man and Woman in that Town were Witches,[50] on Account of several Cattle dying of the present Contagion, great Numbers assembled, some on Horseback, others on Foot, and went, and proclaimed them as such, in three different Market Towns, and about Four in the Afternoon returned to Tring, and demanded the supposed Witches, whom the Inhabitants had sent to the Workhouse for Security, which the enraged Populace being Informed of, went thither,

---

[50] The allegations of witchcraft against Ruth Osborne (1680-1751) and her husband started during the Jacobite Rising of 1745.

*The ducking of Ruth Osborne and her husband at Tring, Herefordshire, England on April 24, 1751.*

and being refused Admittance, they pulled down the greatest Part of the Workhouse and a House adjacent, but the Master in the mean while, having conveyed them to the Vestry of the Church, they afterwards assembled there, obliging the Master of the Workhouse to go with them; they took them out by

Violence, and carried them two Miles from the Town; where they bound the poor Old Woman's Hands and Feet, and after beating her in a cruel and barbarous Manner, threw her into a Pond of Water, where she perished; the old Man was likewise treated in the same Manner.

## *The Virginia Gazette,* Williamsburg, Virginia, November 28, 1751, pg. 2.

*July* 30. At Hereford Assizes was condemned Thomas Colley for the Murder of Ruth Osborne near Tring. The Facts proved at this Trial were as related *Gaz.* No. 29 [July 18, 1751], with the Addition of the following Particulars. Such was the Folly and Superstition of the Crowd, that when they searched the Work-house for the supposed Witch, they looked even into the Salt-box, supposing she might have concealed herself within less Space than would contain a Cat. Having wrapped the deceased and her Husband in two different Sheets, first tying their great Toes and Thumbs together, the most active of the Mob dragged the deceased into the Water by a Cord which they had put round her Body, and she not sinking, the Prisoner Colley went into the Pond, and turned her over several Times with a Stick; after a considerable Time she was hawl'd [hauled] to Shore, and the old Man was dragged into the Pond in the same Manner; and this they repeated to each three Times. The deceased after she was dragg'd [dragged] in the third Time, being pushed about by the Prisoner, flip'd [flipped] out of the Sheet, and her Body was exposed naked; notwithstanding which the Prisoner continued to push her on the Breast with his Stick, which she with her left Hand endeavoured to catch hold of, but was prevented by his snatching it away. After using her in this Manner 'til she was motionless, they dragg'd [dragged] her to Shore, and laid her on the Ground where she expired; and then the Prisoner went among the Spectators, and collected Money of the Pains he had taken in shewing them Sport. The old Man afterwards recovered, but did not appear as an Evidence.

*Colley in ye Marlston Mere turning & Pulling ye poor Woman about and Humbles and Red-Beard holding ye Ropes that they drawed her in by.*

*A period image of Thomas Colley murdering Ruth Osborne.*

## *The Virginia Gazette,* Williamsburg, Virginia, December 5, 1751, pg. 3.

*August* 24. This Day Thomas Colley, for the cruel Murder of Ruth Osborne, on Supposition of her being a Witch, was executed at Gubblecote-Cross, near Marlston-Green, in the Parish of Tring, in Hertfordshire. About 10 on Friday Morning he received the Sacrament at Hereford, administered to him by the Rev. Mr. Edward Bouchier,[51] when he signed a solemn Declaration of his Belief relating to Witchcraft; which he desired might be carried to the Place of Execution, and was there publickly read, at his earnest Request, just before he was turned off, by the Rev. Mr. Randal, Minister of Tring, who attended him in his last Moments. He was escorted by 108 Men belonging to the Regiment of Horse Blue, with their Officers, and two Trumpets; and the Procession was slow, solemn, and moving. Friday Night he was lodged in St. Alban's Goal; at Five the next Morning was put into a One-Horse Chaise, with the Executioner, and came to the Place of Execution about Eleven, and after half an Hour spent in Prayer he was executed, and immediately after hung up in Chains on the same Gibbet he was hanged on. This Infatuation of most of the People in that Part of the Country was such, that they would not be seen near the Place of Execution, insisting that it was a hard Case to hang a Man for destroying an old Woman that had done so much Damage by her Witchcraft. It was said, he was to have been executed a Week sooner, but when the proper Officers came to convey him from the Goal, a prodigious Mob assembled, and would not suffer him to be taken out of Prison.

---

[51] Reverend Edward Bouchier (1707-1775) was the Vicar of All Saints and St. Johns, Hertfordshire, England.

The final words and confessions of criminals were sold as pamphlets in the 18th-century.

*His Declaration, above mentioned, was as follows:*

*Good People,*

I BESEECH you all to take Warning by an unhappy Man's Suffering; that you be not deluded into so absurd and wicked a Conceit, as to believe that there are any such Beings upon Earth as Witches.

It was that foolish and vain Imagination, heightened and inflamed by the Strength of Liquor, which prompted me to be instrumental (with others as mad-brained as myself) in the horrid and barbarous Murder of Ruth Osborne, the supposed Witch, for which I am now so deservedly to suffer Death.

I am fully convinced of my former Error, and with the Sincerity of a dying Man, declare, that I do not believe in such a Thing in being as a Witch; and pray God, that none of you, thro' a contrary Persuasion, may hereafter be induced to think, that you have a Right in any Shape to persecute, much less to endanger the Life of a Fellow-Creature.

I beg of you all to pray to God to forgive me, and to wash clean my polluted Soul in the Blood of Jesus Christ, my Saviour and Redeemer.

So exhorteth you all, the dying
*Thomas Colley.*

THE

# Remarkable CONFESSION,

AND

## Laſt DYING WORDS

OF

# THOMAS COLLEY,

EXECUTED on *Saturday*, *Auguſt* the 24th, 1751,

At GUBBLECUT-CROSS, near *Marlſton* (vulgarly called *Wilſton*) Green, in the Pariſh of *Tring*, in *Hertfordſhire*; and afterwards hung in CHAINS there,

For the cruel MURDER of

# RUTH OSBORNE,

Under Suppoſition of her being a WITCH.

Together with COPIES of ORIGINAL LETTERS which *COLLEY* ſent to his WIFE and FRIENDS during his lying under Condemnation. And a Copy of his ſolemn Declaration of his Faith relating to *Witchcraft*, which was publickly read at the Place of Execution, at his earneſt Requeſt.

*LONDON:*

Printed by R. WALKER, in the *Little Old-Bailey*, and Sold by all Bookſellers and Pamphlet-ſellers in Town and Country.

[ Price Four-Pence. ]

THE

Nunrh. 385.

# MARYLAND GAZETTE,

*Containing the freſheſt Advices foreign and domeſtic.*

THURSDAY, *September* 21, 1752.

## *Maryland Gazette*, Annapolis, Maryland, September 21, 1752, pg. 1.

*Lisbon, May* 1. The King[52] has been so much affected with the Distress which the Inhabitants of Aveira have undergone by frequent Earthquakes and Inundations, that he has granted them as Exemption from all Kinds of Taxes and Impositions for ten Years to come, and has given Orders to furnish them with Provisions at his own Expence. By an Express from Rome there is Advice, that the Pope,[53] at the Intercession of his Majesty, has consented to suppress the annual Procession of the Inquisition,[54] entitled, *The Act of Faith*; in which such unhappy Persons as were accused of Witchcraft or Judaism, used to be made a public Spectacle. His Holiness has also mitigated several other Proceedings of the Inquisition, which were look'd [looked] upon to be too severe.

---

[52] King Joseph I (1714-1777) ruled Portugal from 1750 until his death in 1777.

[53] Pope Benedict XIV (1675-1758) was born Prospero Lorenzo Lambertini and was head of the Catholic Church from 1740 until his death in 1758.

[54] The Portuguese Inquisition started in 1536 and lasted until 1821.

# *Maryland Gazette,* Annapolis, Maryland, March 8, 1753, pg. 2.

Lisbon, Sept. 26.

—*Divers other Persons who were convicted of several Misdemeanors, underwent such Punishments as were thought adequate to the Nature of their Crimes; and as the Notion of Witchcraft is strenuously maintained by some powerful Persons in our Country, five Women, who have been convicted of holding a too familiar Correspondence with the Devil himself, or at least with some of his infernal Ministers, have renounced, in the most solemn Manner imaginable, all such Contracts as they have been supposed to enter into with any of that impious Crew; and nothing surely was ever drawn up in such solemn and particular Terms, as the Interrogatories on which these poor deluded Witches were publicly examined.*

# *The South-Carolina Gazette; and Country Journal,* Charleston, South Carolina, May 26, 1767, pg. 1.

*Extract of a Letter from Genoa, dated January 15.*

# Haunted Land

The Emperor of Germany[55] is now very busy in endeavouring to prevent witchcraft and sorcery, necromancy and juggling. The punishments for those who are detected are different in their degrees of severity; some are even to be punished with death. [*If men and women when they grow old become nearest allayed to the Devil, and more under his direction, will hanging have power enough to prevent it. To be serious, can it be imagined, that in an age so enlightened as the present age is, that a nation like the* Germans *should still retain those idle notions of witchcraft, which did indeed infect the minds of the people of all nations of antiquity, but have long been dismissed from most nations in general in Europe: Notwithstanding among some of the inferior classes, those notions are still retained every where, yet the more enlightened understandings hold them in derision.*]

---

[55] Frederick II the Great (1712-1786) ruled the Kingdom of Prussia from 1740 until his death in 1786.

## *Hartford Courant,* Hartford, Connecticut, November 27, 1769, pg. 2.

Aug. 23. A farmer at Granchester in Cambrigeshire, was bound over to the quarter sessions by the humanity of the Rev. Dr. Plumtree for forcing a poor woman of Caldecot [Caldecote] into the water to prove her a witch, and otherwise maltreating her.

## *The Virginia Gazette,* Williamsburg, Virginia, May 20, 1773, pg. 1.

*March* 12.

A few Days ago, at the Village of Scend [Seend], in Wiltshire, a Report prevailed that a Woman who was dangerously ill of a putrid Fever[56] was bewitched, and this Report excited the Curiosity of Numbers of her Neighbours to go and see her. The Fever attending the dying Person was so high as to render her delirious, and in that State she often cried out, *she is pinching me to Death.* This left it beyond a Doubt, to the credulous Vulgar, that the old Woman, who had long been considered by them as a Witch, was the Cause of her Torment; and near 100 of the *wise* People went to the supposed Witch's House, tied a Rope round her Middle, and carried her to a Mill, where they cruelly gave the old accustomed Discipline of Ducking. On throwing her twice or three Times headlong into the Water, and being unable on Account of her Clothes to keep her under, they were perfectly convinced of her Power of Witchcraft; and supposing this

---

[56] Epidemic typhus

Discipline might be a Means of deterring her from exercising any farther Cruelties to the poor Woman, they suffered her to go home. The poor Woman's Fever, however, increasing, they went again the next Day to the supposed Witch's House, determined to give her another Ducking, but were happily prevented by a Magistrate, who was accidently informed of their Intentions, by whose Means it is probable the poor old Woman escaped falling a Sacrifice to their Resentment.

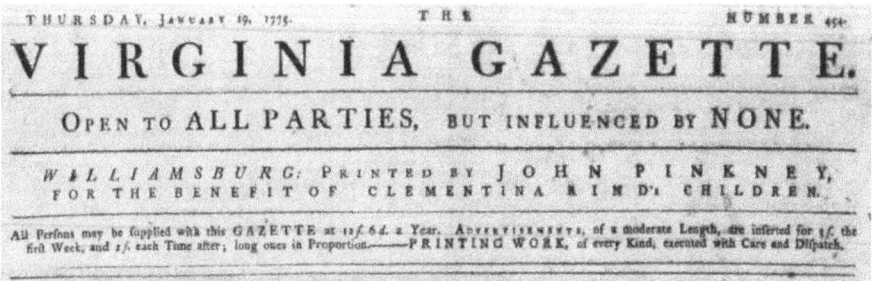

THURSDAY, January 19, 1775.   THE   NUMBER 464.

# VIRGINIA GAZETTE.

OPEN TO ALL PARTIES, BUT INFLUENCED BY NONE.

WILLIAMSBURG: PRINTED BY JOHN PINKNEY, FOR THE BENEFIT OF CLEMENTINA RIND'S CHILDREN.

All Persons may be supplied with this GAZETTE at 12/.6d. a Year. Advertisements, of a moderate Length, are inserted for 3/. the first Week; and 2/. each Time after; long ones in Proportion.——PRINTING WORK, of every Kind, executed with Care and Dispatch.

## *Rind's Virginia Gazette.* Williamsburg, Virginia, January 19, 1775, pg. 1.

Be there not still remaining, in all the land of New England, a prophetess, a cunning old woman, whom men call a witch, and who hath in times past foretold divers things, which have come to pass?

WEDNESDAY, October 3, 1781. [Numb. XXIV.

# THE
# Freeman's Journal:
OR,

North-American

THE

Intelligencer.

OPEN to ALL PARTIES, but INFLUENCED by NONE.

PHILADELPHIA, Printed by FRANCIS BAILEY, in *Market-Street*; between *Third* and *Fourth-Streets*.

## *The Freeman's Journal of The North-American Intelligencer.* Philadelphia, Pennsylvania, October 3, 1781, pg. 3.

Many sensible Englishmen have long surmised that the American revolt is chiefly owing to fascination and witchcraft, it is for this reason we are said to be in a state of delusion. So many of the noble blood have from time to time broke their necks in attempting to break the spell that the king has at last been prevailed upon by an eminent wizard on the other side of the water, to send over one of the blood royal,[57] that by his potent influence he may reduce his majesty's subjects to reason. We apprehend however, he will find it necessary, to return to England and compleat his magical studies, before he can accomplish this desirable purpose. If his royal highness really possesses any such powers, we would advise him for the present, to extend them to Lord

---

[57] Prince William Henry (1765-1837) the future King William IV of England (ruled from 1830-1837). During the American Revolution, Prince William served in New York and was the only member of the royal family to visit America in the 18th-century.

Cornwallis;[58] doubtless that unfortunate gentleman would be content to ride on a broomstick through the air, so he could escape his present embarrassing situation, and perhaps take up Rawdon[59] behind him. — Admiral Digby[60] has also arrived with a fleet — this is very true, and yet — tell it not in Gath[61] — this fleet consists of but three sail of solitary ships — Earl Cornwallis must also be in high spirits, when he reflects upon the present agreeable posture of their affairs. — We leave these worthies to all the ineffable satisfaction they at present are capable of enjoying.

[Many sensible Englishmen have long surmised that the American revolt is chiefly owing to fascination and witchcraft, it is for this reason we are said to be in a state of delusion. So many of the noble blood have from time to time broke their necks in attempting to break the spell that their king has at last been prevailed upon by an eminent wizard on the other side the water, to send over one of the blood royal, that by his potent influence he may reduce his majesty's subjects to reason. We apprehend however, he will find it necessary, to return to England and compleat his magical studies, before he can accomplish this desirable purpose. If his royal highness really possesses any such powers, we would advise him for the present, to extend them to Lord Cornwallis; doubtless that unfortunate gentleman would be content to ride on a broomstick through the air, so he could escape his present embarrassing situation, and perhaps take up Rawdon behind him.— Admiral Digby has also arrived with a fleet—this is very true, and yet—tell it not in Gath—this fleet consists of but three sail of solitary ships—Earl Cornwallis must also be in high spirits, when he reflects upon the present agreeable posture of their affairs.—We leave these worthies to all the ineffable satisfaction they at present are capable of enjoying.]

---

[58] Charles Cornwallis, 1st Marquess Cornwallis (1738-1805) led British forces against George Washington's Continental Army during the American Revolution.

[59] Francis Rawdon-Hastings, 1st Marquess of Hastings (1754-1826) was a British army general who served under Lord Cornwallis.

[60] Robert Digby (1732-1815) was an admiral in the British navy during the American Revolution.

[61] "Tell it not in Gath, Proclaim it not in the streets of Ashkelon—Lest the daughters of the Philistines rejoice, Lest the daughters of the uncircumcised triumph" (2 Samuel 1:20). Gath was a city-state of the Philistines.

JANUARY, 1785.  THE  Numb. 17.

# INDEPENDENT GAZETTEER;

## OR, THE

## CHRONICLE OF FREEDOM.

That the People have a Right to Freedom of Speech, and of writing, and publishing their Sentiments; therefore the Freedom of the Press ought not to be restrained.——PENNSYLVANIA BILL OF RIGHTS.

Let it be impressed upon your Minds——let it be instilled into your Children, that the Liberty of the Press is the PALLADIUM of all the civil, political, and religious Rights of FREEMEN.——JUNIUS.

1785.  SATURDAY, January 29.  Price Six Pence.

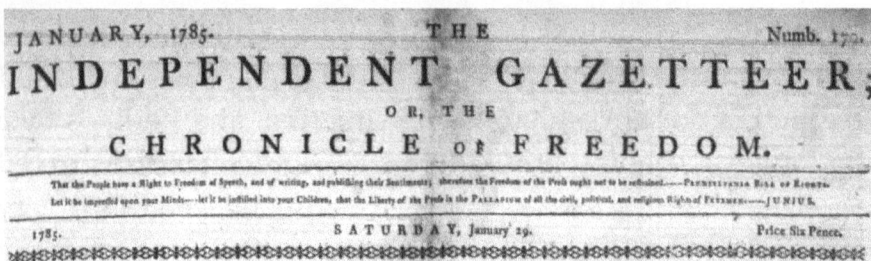

## *The Independent Gazetteer,* Philadelphia, Pennsylvania, January 29, 1785, pg. 2.

Foreign Intelligence.

HAGUE, November 5.

The ancient severity of the inquisition is greatly relaxed in the Catholic countries in Europe. An event that lately took place at Bologna is a proof of this: A man of 60 years of age, by trade a potter, who had been convicted before that tribunal of witchcraft and holding converse with the devil, was paraded through the streets sitting on an ass, with a label affixed to his breast, signifying his crime, and after being carried through the principal parts of the town, he was set at liberty without any other punishment. He had been in the prisons of the

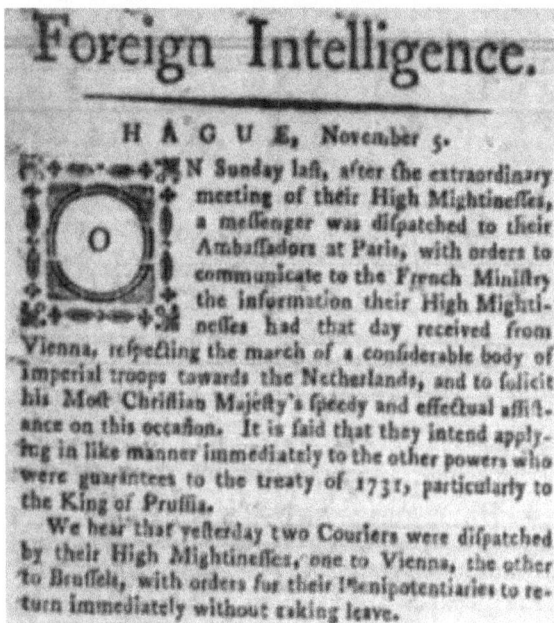

inquisition only nine months, during which time he had not been put to the torture ordinary and extraordinary above once a month.

> The ancient severity of the inquisition is greatly relaxed in the Catholic countries in Europe. An event that lately took place at Bologna is a proof of this : A man of 60 years of age, by trade a potter, who had been convicted before that tribunal of witchcraft and holding converse with the devil, was paraded through the streets sitting on an ass, with a label affixed to his breast, signifying his crime, and after being carried through the principal parts of the town, he was set at liberty without any other punishment. He had been in the prisons of the inquisition only nine months, during which time he had not been put to the torture ordinary and extraordinary above once a month.

## *The Pennsylvania Packet,* Philadelphia, Pennsylvania, June 28, 1785, pg. 2.

Extract of a letter from Falmouth, April 12.

At a time when some four-footed animals are taught to equal, if not exceed, the human race in the deep sciences, it must give you pleasure to hear of a new importation of the most extraordinary nature, and to which I am an eye-witness, otherwise you might doubt the authenticity of the following information. Just arrived here with crowded sails the brig Nostra Seiguiora de Magdalena, from Lisbon; she narrowly escaped a light frigate sent after her, with a number of officers of the holy inquisition on board, in order to bring the freighters, &c. dead or alive, before the dreadful tribunal, on suspicion of witchcraft, or as the warrant declares, for having entered into express compact with the devil and his angels.

73

Emanuel Pedro de Silva, proprietor of the animals, makes the following declaration, "that though the defendant of a noble and rich family in Portugal, yet by the earthquake at Lisbon,[62] and other causes, he was obliged early in life to shift for himself, and to turn ass and mule driver between Lisbon and Madrid; that by a long acquaintance with the docility of these animals, he at his leisure taught them what was deemed supernatural in Portugal, and of consequence brought down the wrath of the holy inquisition on him. Death in the most cruel manner would have been his lot, if fortunately he had not made escape to this land of freedom. Emanuel Pedro de Silva has brought over with him seven large asses, of the true dapple breed, from Salamanco, and declares with confidence, that one of them shall play any piece of music put before him on the piano forte, equal to the most expert Italian performer; another tells fortunes to the life; a third finds out stolen goods; a fourth touches the fandango on the harp, and the rest dance to time; the fifth blows the French horn incomparably; the sixth and seventh dance to a miracle on the tight rope."

---

[62] The Great Lisbon earthquake occurred on November 1, 1755, on the Feast of All Saints. The earthquake was an estimated 8.5-9.0 magnitude and caused fires and a tsunami and killed an estimated 30,000 people.

*An 18th-century engraving of the Lisbon, Portugal earthquake of 1755.*

## *Hartford Courant,* Hartford, Connecticut, November 28, 1785, pg. 3

*LITCHFIELD, November* 15.

Last Wednesday *Thomas Goss,* late of *Berkhamsted* [Barkhamsted], was executed at this place, pursuant to the sentence of the Superior Court, for the murder of his wife.— His defense, upon trial, was *Insanity;* and for the space of several days after his trial and condemnation, but appeared regular, and requested his Attorney to make application to the General Assembly of the State, for a reprieve: likewise desired the Clergyman of this town to preach a sermon at his execution, (if he were not reprieved.) But very soon he resumed his former notions, that wizards and witches haunted him; which ideas it seems he had adopted, some time in October 1784; and under pretense that his wife was a witch, he at first justified his conduct in depriving her of life.—Under such infatuation, he ordered his Attorney, in most peremptory language, not to apply for a reprieve to any human tribunal; alleging that his heavenly Father had forbidden all such proceedings.—He called himself the second Lamb of God: said he was brother of Jesus Christ; and sometimes said, he was the child, born of the woman, mentioned in the Revelations of St. John, before whom the dragon stood, ready to devour the child, &c—To such extravagant ideas, he added, that the Sheriff could not hang him; that his heavenly Father would interpose if the attempt were made, and he be liberated; and that thirty thousand males above fifteen years of age, would be instantly killed by the shock, in North America.—He pertinaciously adhered to such wild opinions to the last moment of his life.—The night preceding his execution he slept well.—In the forenoon of the same day, slept calmly a considerable length of time:—at dinner, ate heartily.—On his way to the gallows, and while there, he appeared calm and unmoved; not the least emotion could be discerned in his countenance; nor the least perturbation in his speech.—On being told he had but twenty minutes to live, he kneeled down, and made a short prayer, and consented that a Clergyman present should pray with him, (altho' [although] he had refused his attention to either preaching or praying, and would not even hear the sermon preached on the day of his execution, pretending that God forbade him.)—When on the gallows, he said a few words to the spectators, inculcating the general principles of morality; such as that they ought to bring up their families well, and obey the precepts of his heavenly Father, or they must be miserable—He declared he never murdered any person in his life, excepting his wife; and the last word he said, was, that he believed that the Sheriff could not hang him!

[Vol. IV.]  No. 40  THE  [Num. 104.]

# VERMONT JOURNAL,

## AND THE

# UNIVERSAL ADVERTISER.

MONDAY,  JUNE 25, 1787.

WINDSOR; Printed by HOUGH and SPOONER.

*From Realms far distant, and from Climes unknown, We make the Knowledge of Mankind your own.*

## *The Vermont Journal,* Windsor, Vermont, June 25, 1787, pg. 2.

PHILIDELPHIA, May 6.

*May* 14.—An ancient woman residing near the New-market in this city, whose name is not at present recollected, was treated exceedingly ill by some persons of the vicinity, on Saturday last.  Upon a supposition that was a *witch*, she was cut in the forehead, according to *ancient* and *immemorial* custom, by those persons: This old body long since laboured under suspicions of sorcery, and was viewed as the pest and night mare of society in those parts of the town where she has hitherto lived; she was commonly called at Spring Garden, Korbmacher,[63] by the Germans; and on that score on the present and other occasions, unfortunately became the victim of vengeance of some individuals, who afforded her the most pointed abuse which so mistaken a passion and resentment could possibly impose and inflict.

As she has now appealed to the laws of her country for protection and countenance, apprehending her life in danger,

---

[63] Korbmacher is German for a wicker worker or a basket maker.

it must be the wish of every liberal character, that the absurd and abominable notions of witch-craft and sorcery, will no more predominate in a country like ours, that has emancipated itself from the superstitions of authority, and in fact every other species of superstitions, consisting in the bondage of the body, and the mind! The doctrine of witches, ghosts and faries, continues our correspondent, has obtained too general a prevalence in the old world, insomuch, in many remarkable influences, (is mournful story) that it has been productive of the mischievous effects imaginable. Let us not adopt these principles in the free and civilized parts of independent America, which has no good reason to boast like the famous foil of Endor!

The dispensation of Providence is very little felt or understood in the days of Ignorance, or in young and infant countries, and 'tis generally observed, never doth wickedness and cruelty so much abound as in dark and gloomy times. Far from indulging proper notions that the 'great governor of the world'[64] concludes himself by general laws, which are inflexible, because the best possible, every trivial event is attributed to the Almighty and commanding power. Yet, to suppose any man or woman should have absolute dominion to annoy and injure their fellow creatures, and make them miserable 'at will and pleasure,' is undoubtedly impious to an

---

[64] "And Whereas it hath pleased the Great Governor of the World to incline the hearts of the legislatures we respectively represent in Congress, to approved of, and to authorize us to ratify the said Articles of Confederation and perpetual Union" (Articles of Confederation, Article XIII). The Article of Confederation, ratified on March 1, 1781, was an agreement to establish a national government among the original thirteen states of the United States. The Articles proved to be weak and were replaced by the Constitution of the United States. The attack on the unnamed woman occurred in Philadelphia while the Constitutional Convention was being held in Independence Hall and reflected the heightened political and social instability of the Confederation era.

extreme, and at once removing God himself from his exulted station in the celestial system and arrangement of affairs!

A belief so horrid is a picture of the greatest weakness in human nature, and can only source from a mind closed up in its scanty orbit, replete with dormant prejudices, and thick with the grossest original ignorance.

It would deprive us of our hopes and fears, of our pleasures and serious anxieties, and leave nothing to contemplate upon, nor any positive end to pursue—it would destroy our free agency and activity, the offsprings of the divinity itself, and reduce man to a passive, inanimate and stupid being; in fine, it would controul the grand course of providence, and abuse the sacred and sublime decrees of Heaven, which have directed man (if he chooses) like Mary of old, to take the better part and be both sociable and happy.[65]

Absurd opinions, those of so dismal complexion should be surrendered at the eyes of superstitious have opened and owned its errors, from instruction, experience and civilization. But prejudices, worm-eaten prejudices, as our old companions, are hard to be parted with.

---

[65] This is a reference to the biblical story of Mary and Martha in Luke 10:38-42. Two sisters, Mary and Martha, welcomed Jesus and his disciples into their home. While Martha became distracted by making her guests comfortable, Mary chose to sit at Jesus' feet and listen to his teachings. Martha became irritated by Mary's behavior and asked Jesus to chastise her. To which Jesus replied, "Martha, Martha, thou art careful and troubled about many things: But one thing is needful: and Mary hath chosen thou good part, which shall not be taken away from her" (Luke: 10:41-42).

## *The Independent Gazetteer,* Philadelphia, Pennsylvania, July 16, 1787, pg. 3.

*Extract of a letter from Dublin, dated April 26.*

We are sorry to hear that the poor old woman who suffered so much, some time ago, under the imputation of being *a witch*, has again been attacked by an ignorant and inhuman mob. On Tuesday last she was carted through several of the streets, and was hooted and pelted as she passed along. A gentleman who interfered in her favour was greatly insulted, whist those who recited the innumerable instances of her art, were listened to with curiosity and attention. The repetition of this outrage calls for the serious interposition of the officers of government, not merely for the sake of the wretched object herself (though surely she has a peculiar claim to the protection of the law) but for the sake of the illiterate and youthful part of society, who will naturally imagine that the charge of sorcery must be just, when such persecution is publicly practiced with impunity. It is with pleasure we add, that several respectable citizens, who were present, have determined to bear testimony against these violators of tranquility and common sense, and that a gentleman of the law has voluntarily undertaken the prosecution.

## *The Independent Gazetteer,* Philadelphia, Pennsylvania, October 29, 1787, pg. 2.

*Philadelphia, October 29.*

On Monday last the city sessions commenced, and on Friday the business of the court was concluded. Several persons were condemned to the wheel-barrow, but the greater number of bills were for keeping disorderly houses, and committing assaults and battery—a melancholy proof of the depraved manners, and the contentious spirit of the times. One woman, who had been indicted for some violence offered to the person of the unhappy creature that was lately attacked by a mob under the imputation of being a witch, maintained the justice of that opinion, and insinuated her belief that her only child sickened and died, under the malignant influence of a *charm*. Upon which the presiding justice made the following observation—"What! that a poor wretch whose sorrows and infirmities have sunk her eyes into her head, and whose features are streaked with the wrinkles of extreme old age, should therefore become an object of terror, and be endowed with the powers of witchcraft—it is an idle and absurd superstition! If however some damsels that I have seen, animated with the bloom of youth, and equipped with all the grace of beauty, if such women were indicted for the offence, the charge might receive some countence, for they are indeed calculated to *charm* and *bewitch* us. But age and infirmity, though they deserve our compassion, have nothing in them that can alarm or fascinate our nature."

## *Hartford Courant,* Hartford, Connecticut, December 8, 1788, pg. 2.

A few days since a lady, with an immense circumference of bottom, as she was stepping into a boat at Black fiar's Bridge, by the awkwardness of the waterman in handing her off of the stairs, lost her footing, and tumbled into the Thames; but instead of sinking, to the surprise of every body, from her hips up, she appeared above water; all the boats immediately put out after her; but the wind and tide both going strongly down the river, added to an immense parachute hat she had on, acting as a sail, there was no overtaking her; in this most seemingly perilous state, the poor lady proceeded like a mairmaid [mermaid], till the alarm became so general on the river, that the combined fleets of the old Swan, and Tower Stairs, put out all the navies, and luckily meeting her as she passed London Bridge, towed her safely into Billingsgate; but her fright did not end here, for as she was stricken in years, and her dip in the Thames having resorted her shriveled countenance to its native sallow, the ladies of Billingsgate, with one united voice, pronounced her a WITCH; nor could she have escaped their fury, if she had not *proved*, to the satisfaction of these conscientious matrons,

THE BUM SHOP.

*A 1780s satirical print parodying the fashionable false rumps.*

that it was not to the DEVIL, but to a CORK RUMP,[66] she owed her safety.

## *The Maryland Gazette,* Annapolis, Maryland, April 9, 1789, pg. 1.

LANSINGBURGH, *March* 23.
*Extract of a letter from Poughkeepsie, March* 9.

"The late surprising occurrence at Dr. Thorn's, in New-Hackinsack, will, I believe, in some degree, re-establish the opinion, that there has been, and still is, such a thing as wizards and witches, notwithstanding the idea has been long thrown aside by even the vulgar. You have doubtless heard the story of that unfortunate girl—the sad disaster which has befallen her excites the curiosity of every one, and numbers are constantly flocking to see her, from twenty miles round. Scare a stage passes, without stopping at the doctor's, although he lives several miles from the main road. The neighbouring divines attend her constantly—they minute the most essential part of what occurs daily, and will, perhaps, commit it to the press. Many ways have been tried to relieve her from the agitated state in which she appears, but to no purpose; the knocking still continues, accompanied with a rumbling noise, and moving of the furniture. It is supposed by some, that she is bewitched by a Hessian servant of the doctor's, whose conduct for some time past has been very singular; he was lately brought to an examination, on which

---

[66] False rumps were worn in the 1780s to support long trains worn by fashionable ladies. The rumps were stuffed with horse hair, cotton ticking, and cork.

occasion his behaviour greatly heightened the suspicion; since then his precipitate departure seems to confirm it."

## General Advertiser, Philadelphia, Pennsylvania, November 24, 1792, pg. 3.

COLUMBIA (S. C.) November 10.

Notwithstanding the salutary laws enacted in this state for the preservation of the public peace, the most flagrant and violent outrages have recently been committed in the Fairfield county. The perpetrators of the facts alluded to are those who, under the cloak of religious opinions, and willfully blinded by the nefarious doctrines of some ignorant and unprincipled teachers, have been led to the commission of the most atrocious crimes; and, with the plausible pretext of serving the lord, have conceived there was no way of doing it so effectually as by dispatching the aged & infirm post haste to heaven. A number of wretches have beaten and abused a man about eighty years old, and two women who both exceed that age, because they happened to possess more sense than their neighbours and were otherwise strikingly distinguished from them by their inoffensive conduct and the purity of their morals. These remarkable singularities gave rise to a pretended belief that they were agents of the Devil, that they were guilty of the sin of witchcraft, and they were treated accordingly: after whipping them in a most shocking manner, hot coals were applied to their extremities, till signs of life were scarcely discernible. In this dreadful situation the barbarians left them to the mercy of that God alone, in whose hands are the issues of life and death, and who will not fail in his just wrath to hurl perdition on this infernal tribe of hypocrites. There cannot be any doubt that proper steps will be taken to bring these superstitious bigots to condign punishment. Their number is said to amount nearly to 50, and they have associated themselves together in order to oppose the officers of justice, should they attempt to apprehend them; we cannot, however, help indulging a wish, that speedy and exemplary vengeance may overtake their crimes; and that they may, by a sincere repentance of their transgressions, obtain that mercy at the throne of Grace, which, in common humanity to their fellow creatures, ought to be denied them here.

The Lancaster Journal.

NOT TOO RASH—YET NOT FEARFUL—OPEN TO ALL PARTIES,—BUT NOT INFLUENCED BY ANY.
HERE TRUTH UNLICENS'D REIGNS; AND DARES ACCOST E'EN KINGS THEMSELVES AND RULERS OF THE FREE.

LANCASTER: Printed by WILLIAM HAMILTON, at Franklin's Head, in King-Street, the Easternmost of Mr. Stoffi's new Houses, and next Door to Mr. Michael Riue, at the low Price of Two Dollars per Annum. Advertisements, Essays, and Articles of Intelligence thankfully received, and every kind of Printing executed with Accuracy and Dispatch.

No. 48.]                    F R I D A Y, December 23; 1796.                    [Vol. III.

**Lancaster Intelligencer and Journal, Lancaster, Pennsylvania, December 23, 1796, pg. 3.**

It almost transcends belief that the close of the 18th century, in a civilized country, a human being should be cruelly & personally ill-treated on a charge of witchcraft. The fact is, that, at the late court of common pleas and general sessions, held at Biddeford, for the county of York, Massachusetts, an action was commenced on behalf of the commonwealth, for an assault and battery on Elizabeth Smith. In the course of the trial, it appeared the complainant

It almoſt tranſcends belief that at the cloſe of the 18th century, in a civilized country, a human being ſhould be cruelly & perſonally ill-treated on a charge of witch-craft. The fact is, that, at the late court of common pleas and general ſeſſions, hold-en at Biddeford, for the county of York, Maſſachuſetts, an action was commenced on behalf of the commonwealth, for an aſ-fault and battery on Elizabeth Smith. In the courſe of the trial, it appeared the complainant had been accuſed of witch-craft, and that not only her neighbours, but her relations, had been ſo incenſed a-gainſt her, that ſhe had been obliged to flee to a neighbouring town for ſafety.—a man named Hilton became inſane in October laſt, and in that ſtate accuſed the complai-nant of bewitching him, alledging that as he was going home one evening, himſelf being then in a ſound ſtate of mind, the complainant walked before him, and he felt an ox goad which he held in his hand, move through it, but that, convinced the com-plainant did it, he drew it back and ſtruck her, but inſtead of doing her any injury, he received a violent blow on the lower part of his back, which gave him exceſſive pain.

had been accused of witchcraft, and that not only her neighbours, but her relations, had been obliged to flee to a neighbouring town for safety.—A man named Hilton became insane in October last, and in that state accused the complainant of bewitching him, alleging that as he was going home one evening, himself being then in a sound state of mind, the complainant walked before him, and he felt an ox goad which he held in his hand, move through it, but that, convinced the complainant did it, he drew it back and struck her, but instead of doing her any injury, he received a violent blow on the lower part of his back, which gave him excessive pain. Witnesses were produced to corroborate this—and also that the complainant had been requested to visit him which she did, and also consented to be let blood as an antidote. The infatuated people about Hilton persisted in saying that she bewitched him, and that they would not him loose, (he being then insane) to kill her; whether by chance or design he did escape, and the poor creature's life nearly paid the forfeit, whilst his niece urged him on to kill her.—They, to use their own words, used "many projects" to destroy her, which failed. The delusion appeared to be general, and the profound ignorance of the people gave a very serious aspect of the business.—

Judge Wells however, endeavoured to weed their minds from this gross and mischievous error, and the parties were bound to keep the peace till August next.

## *General Advertiser.* Philadelphia. Pennsylvania. September 25, 1792, pg. 2.

*MAGICAL INCANTATION.*
[*From a London Paper.*]

A farmer in Aldenham, near Watford, in Hertfordshire, who a few weeks since had observed some unusual symptoms in a mare, which eluded the skill of the farrier, was advised by his neighbours to have her shot; but so it happened, that no sooner was the fatal tube got ready, than the animal appeared perfectly well, and another mare was seized with the disorder, in reality nothing more than the staggers[67] — This sudden transition was immediately deemed *witchcraft* by the farmer's wife, and some of her companions of which had such an effect upon the good man, that he was easily persuaded to procure some of its urine, and to mix it with a number of crooked pins, which being close corked up in a bottle, was to be set on the fire till the supposed witch should come to the house! These directions were strictly attended to; but on the increase of heat, the vessel not only burst with a loud explosion, but some of the pieces were so forcibly driven into the face of the observers, that they have not yet been able to appear in public, without undergoing the laugh of the village; yet, what tends the more to confirm them

---

[67] The staggers also called the grass staggers in horses is generally caused by a mineral imbalance in rapid growth grass in the Autumn. The symptoms of the grass staggers is that the horse has an uncoordinated gait and is easily treated by removing the horse from the effected pasture.

in their superstitious is, that neither of the horses have had a single fit since the ceremony was performed.

## *The Independent Gazetteer.* Philadelphia. Pennsylvania. November 23. 1793. pg. 2.

We learn that a negro man, the property of Mr. Green, in the state of N. Carolina, was tried a fortnight ago for *witchcraft!* before two magistrates and several freeholders, who condemned him to be hanged; and he was accordingly executed in a very short time afterwards. He was appraised at seventy pounds.
[*Charleston Gaz.*].

THE FARMERS' LIBRARY:
Or, Vermont Political & Historical Register.

No. 38. of Vol. I.     MONDAY, December 16, 1793.     Whole No. 38.

A Political & Historical Paper, by J. LYON, Published every Monday near the State House, Rutland.

—The FREEDOM and IMPARTIALITY of the PRESS shall remain INVIOLATE.—

## *The Farmer's Library; or, Vermont Political & Historical Register.* Rutland. Vermont. December 16. 1793. pg. 2.

I OBSERVED in your last, under the New Jersey head, an account of the trial and execution of a Negro, in North Carolina for Witchcraft.—Since the delusive mist of kingcraft and priestcraft, hath been so eradicated by the sunshine of enlightened liberty, who could have expected that again the fabulous notion of witchcraft could have gained so much credit in this enlightened age and country as judiciarly to have taken the life of a poor African. *Tell it not in Gath, Publish it not in Askelon,* let it be banished, let it never disgrace the annals of an American state.—And after we have pitied and forgiven those who have made this African sacrifice, to their deluded ignorance, may their memory forever, ever be forgotten.

## *The Rutland Herald: A Register of the Times,* Rutland, Vermont, October 23, 1797, pg. 1.

Jemmy Twitcher is a venerable descendent of the ancient family of Twitchers, which emigrated to this country, and settled in Massachusetts about 1630. His ancestors believed in witchcraft; & about the time the witches were so troublesome as to get themselves hanged they cut up a pewter plate into a variety of curious anti-witch figures which they wore suspended on their arms, and breast: by which means they escaped the influence of witches, as effectually as we now fears away the yellow fever,[68] with bags of camphor hung under the nose.[69]

These pieces of pewter, Jemmy Twitcher has received from his great grand father; and being long preserved as heirlooms in the eldest branch of the family, they are considered as venerable as the relics of a saint. Old Jemmy

---

[68] Outbreaks of yellow fever was common in the 1790s, the disease was particularly dreaded during this period as the cause of the disease had not been determined. The worst outbreak of yellow fever was in Philadelphia in the summer and fall of 1793 when an estimated 5,000 died.

[69] Bags of camphor were hung around the neck as a preventive for yellow fever.

keeps them suspended in one corner of his parlor, which is well furnished otherwise in the modern style.

The stranger who enters the room, and admires and praises the carpet, the paper hangings,[70] the curtains, or the mahogany, is heard without an emotion; and if he leaves the room without espying the pewter figures, Jemmy sets him down for a rustic blockhead. But let him hit upon the witch fenders, which guarded his ancestors from the fury of the witches, and Jemmy is as *tickled* as a child; he praises the man's taste, and good sense—begs he will call again—and the best he has shall be at his service.—The only thing is to find the point where a man can be *tickled*. Reader, hast thou thy ticklish spot?—Thou wilt hear from me.

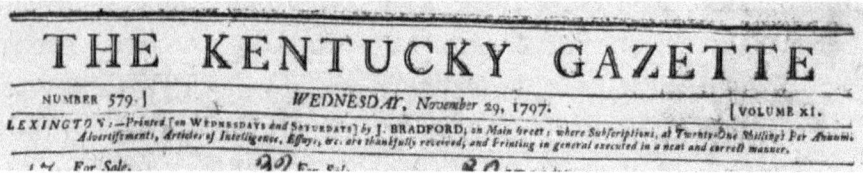

THE KENTUCKY GAZETTE

NUMBER 579. ]    WEDNESDAY, November 29, 1797.    [ VOLUME XI.

LEXINGTON.—Printed [on WEDNESDAYS and SATURDAYS] by J. BRADFORD; on Main Street; where Subscriptions, at Twenty-One Shillings Per Annum. Advertisements, Articles of Intelligence, Essays, &c. are thankfully received; and Printing in general executed in a neat and correct manner.

## Kentucky Gazette, Lexington, Kentucky, November 8, 1797, pg. 4.

WITCHCRAFT
A VIRGINIA ANECDOTE.

About the year 1727, when the back settlers of this country were as proverbial for their prejudices as ever the first settlers of Plymouth were, an old woman about 120 miles from Richmond, on James river, was so unfortunate as to have a sow litter a pig with two tails. This circumstance soon overran the settlement. A general alarm was spread; and the

---

[70] Wallpaper

parson of the Parish was resorted to by the affrighted people to account for this wonderful phenomenon. The sage divine, after duly considering the affair, declared, that as all pigs by nature were endowed with but one tail, it was probable that the devil was officious in the generation of this litter, and as he cannot make any thing perfect, these two tails were left as a mark of his imperfection. The parson further observed, that as other neighbours had sows, on whom the evil spirit might have tried his operations, his partiality for this old woman was a proof that she must have a connection with him, and that she could be nothing less than a witch. The poor woman was immediately apprehended and it was determined to tie her up in a sack and throw her into the river, when if she floated she was a witch, and must be hung; if she sunk then she was innocent. A vast concourse of people assembled on the banks to see the operation; and while the church wardens were absolutely engaged in drawing the bag over her, a Col. Taylor, who was lately arrived from Ireland, hit on the following stratagem to save her:

"By my soul (said he to the wardens) ye are all wrong; you know nothing of witches; now in Ireland, we have found out a much surer way without half the trouble": the people were anxious to hear the Irish method: "why (says the colonel) my jewels, we put the woman in one scale and the big church bible in the other: if the bible outweighs the woman, she is a witch, and must be burnt; but if the woman is the heaviest, she is no witch by my soul." The col's method was approved of: the trial made; and thus the life of a woman preserved, who, but for Col. Taylor's stratagem, must have fallen a sacrifice to the ignorance of an illiterate people.

## *Spooner's Vermont Journal,* Windsor, Vermont, March 14, 1798, pg. 1.

Men employ witches, wizards, conjurers, diviners, and the whole group of fools and numbskulls, just as people employ empirics and mountebanks,[71] with great hopes, and the most sanguine expectations. Their fancies effect much more than the wizard or the quack.

## *Green Mountain Patriot,* Peacham, Vermont, May 25, 1798, pg. 4.

From the FARMER'S WEEKLY MUSEUM.
The PEDLAR.
WITCHCRAFT.

WHEN a boy, I well remember, that scarcely a week passed without hearing some notable tale of recent witchcraft. But at this day we hardly hear such a tale once a month. *Then* there were at least four able bodied witches to a town; but *now*, scarcely one can be mustered; nay, I know of several whole towns with not a single witch in them. *Then* if a teamster had his sled or wheels upset, the nearest witch was sure to bare the blame of it; but now he is forced to lay it off upon a rock, a stump, or a snow drift. In those days if a man was taken out of his warm bed and ridden a hundred miles

---

[71] A person who cheats another out of money.

*From the* FARMER'S WEEKLY MUSEUM.

The PEDLAR.

WITCHCRAFT.

WHEN a boy, I well remember, that scarcely a week passed without hearing some notable tale of recent witchcraft. But at this day we hardly hear such a tale once a month. Then there were at least four able bodied witches to a town; but now, scarcely one can be mustered; nay, I know of several whole towns with not a single witch in them. Then if a teamster had his sled or wheels upset, the nearest witch was sure to bare the blame of it; but now he is forced to lay it off upon a rock, a stump, or a snow drift. In those days if a man was taken out of his warm bed and ridden a hundred miles through the air, it was certainly some old witch who did it; *now* it is turned off upon a dream, a disturbed imagination, or at best, the night mare. If a boy then got into *an odd sort of a way,* using contortions, grimaces, or other singular gesture or movements, he was sure to be bewitched; whereas it is now nothing more than the hypo, Saint Vitus's dance,[72] or some such disorder. These cases and contrasts are asserted as matters of fact; and are mentioned partly to shew how witchcraft has decreased for these last five and thirty years, and partly how those who remain are notoriously degenerated; so that for the matter of exploits they do, we might as well be without them.

I have lately heard of an old man (who, by the bye, had always a singular set of ideas) who laments this decrease and degeneracy; and is disturbed lest the rising generation,

---

[72] Sydenham's chorea is the medical name for Saint Vitus' dance. The disorder is characterized by rapid, uncoordinated jerking movements in the face, hands, and feet.

having nothing to fear, will be under no sort of house government. He has lately gone to reside with a son of his whom he had by his last wife. This son has a house full of boys unruly, untamed, undisciplined: The old man says it is all owning to witches. I believe the fact I have stated, (the decrease of witches,) will be allowed on all hands; but the cause of it is another matter. A friend of mine accounts for it by way of *gunpowder and politics*; and goes on to explain, that it was most rapid in the time of the American war; between that and the year eighty nine,[73] he says, it met with a little check; but again took a new start when the war broke out in Europe.[74] Though I could not deny that there was some truth in what he said about its decrease in the time of our war, yet it occurring that it was directly the contrary all the while the Indian muskets were popping round us, I could not agree that *gunpowder* (however it might be with *politics*) had any hand in it. No, I hereby declare it as my opinion that this decrease is owning to another cause.

"Every generation grows *wiser and wiser;*" I will add *better and better*—and—not a word more.

---

[73] 1789 was a significant year in the history of the United States and France. On April 30, 1789, George Washington became the first president of the United States of America under the Constitution. Three months later on July 14, 1789, the French Revolution began with the Storming of the Bastille.

[74] The political instability of the French Revolution sparked a series of conflicts known as the French Revolutionary Wars (1792-1802) between France and the major powers of Europe.

# Chapter III

## Fortune Tellers

Fortune tellers have been relied upon since ancient times. The Oracle of Delphi were famous in the Greco-Roman world for their accurate predictions. With the rise of Christianity, fortune tellers were also lumped in with witchcraft as evil and something that had to be eradicated. Despite the mandates against fortune telling, people still found ways to practice their craft.

The most common form of fortune telling in the 18th-century was palm reading. This was an easy way to tell a person's future by analyzing the lines on a person's hand and did not require the fortune teller to be literate. Palm readers tending to be gypsy women who traveled around the countryside reading fortunes for a small fee. If a professional fortune teller was not available, young ladies could read their fortunes using regular playing cards, tarot cards, or with specially printed "conversation cards."

## *The Pennsylvania Gazette,* Philadelphia, Pennsylvania, May 25-June 1, 1732, pg. 3.

*London, Feb.* 23. They write from Lansworney in Glamorganshire [Wales], That a poor Fellow of that Place hanged himself there a few Days ago, the Cause of which was very whimsical; It seems he had for some Years past set up for a Fortune-teller among the Vulgar, and to gain himself the more Repute in the Knowledge of Astrology, pretended to foretell the Year, Month, Day, and Hour of his Death; but happening to continue in perfect Health to the Time, and fearing he should be banter'd [bantered] if he outliv'd [outlived] it, he chose to dispatch himself as aforementioned, in order to verify the Prediction.

## *The Pennsylvania Gazette,* Philadelphia, Pennsylvania, May 30, 1751, pg. 3.

*ON the 2d of this inst. the house of Mary Clayton,[75] in Chichester, in the county of Chester, near Marcus-book, widow, was robbed by an Egyptian[76] woman call'd [called] Mary, who had a male child with her, about 2 years old, she was meanly cloathed; the robbery consisted of Ten Pounds Two Shillings and Six-pence, all in Dollars, and one pair of new gold buttons, to the value of One Pound Eighteen Shillings, and a homespun worked gown, of a moss colour, and blue, a shift, and 2 aprons, a striped petticoat, of linsey woolsey: She was seen at Germantown on the 20th past, and passes for a fortune teller, and had the forementioned gown with her.*

---

[75] Mary Martin Clayton (c. 1688-1759) was born in Wiltshire, England and died in Exton, Pennsylvania.

[76] Gypsy

*Whoever secures said robber in any goal* [jail] *where she may be brought to justice, shall receive* Forty Shillings *as a reward, and reasonable charges, paid by me, or* Martin Reardon, *Saddler, in Chestnut-street, Philadelphia.*

*A 18th-century fortune teller.*

## *The Pennsylvania Gazette,* Philadelphia, Pennsylvania, March 12, 1767, pg. 3.

*RUN away from the subscriber, the 28th of February, living in Pine-street, near the New-market, a servant woman, named Judith Bolton, it is likely she will change her name to Philips, as she told several that was her name; she is a little short woman, stoops much in her shoulders, has fair hair, large full eyes, a sort of hazel colour; she had on, when she went away, an old long camblet cloak, faced before with old green shalloon, and has a large hole burnt in*

*the bottom, just at the back seam, a lincey [linsey] petticoat, with brown, white, blue red and yellow stripes in it, an old country cloth jacket, patched under the arms, a blue and white bird-eyed cotton handkerchief, a pair of leather shoes, trod very much aside. She pretends to be a great fortune-teller, is a very hard drinker, and has been many years in the army with the soldiers. Whoever takes up the said servant, and brings her home, or secures her in any goal [jail], so that she may be had again, shall have TWENTY SHILLINGS reward, besides reasonable charges, paid by me*
ELIZABETH ROBERTSON.

The Pennſylvania Packet, *and Daily Advertiſer.*

Price Four-Pence.]          SATURDAY, JULY 23, 1785.          [No. 2017.

## *The Pennsylvania Packet,* Philadelphia, Pennsylvania, July 23, 1785, pg. 2.

LONDON.
*May 14.*

Our fair country woman, who was to have shewn her *heroism* in ascending yesterday[77] while the *dexterous* and *experienced* Lunardi,[78] and the English *philosopher* his companion, is a certain celebrated fortune-teller of Store Street, Tottenham-Court road. This lady, having consulted the planetary influence of the day, found it unfavourable to the ascension, and the *bold fugitive* determined to defer her *celestial sensations* to some happier opportunity. One of the

---

[77] Letitia Anne Sage (c. 1750-1817) was the first English woman to ride in a hot air balloon. She published her account of the voyage in a pamphlet *A Letter, Addressed to a Female Friend, By Mrs. Sage, the First Female Aerial Traveller* (1785).

[78] Vincenzo Lunardi (1754-1806) was a pioneering Italian aeronaut.

gentlemen she prevailed upon to relinquish the enterprize; but the scientific Lunardi, holding judicial astrology in too much contempt, persisted in his resolution of ascending, and saw his error too late, when the balloon run foul of the unfortunate chimney that caused its catastrophe.

*Letitia Anne Sage, Vincenzo Lunardi, and George Biggin ascend in a hot air balloon in 1785 (The British Museum, 1868,0808.2421)*

## *The Pennsylvania Packet,* Philadelphia, Pennsylvania, July 1, 1786, pg. 2.

NEW-LONDON, June 22.

Died. Lilly, a negro woman of great eminences as a fortune teller, and as such well known to the privateers of this port in the late war.

## *The Pennsylvania Packet,* Philadelphia, Pennsylvania, July 15, 1790, pg. 3.

ANECDOTE.

ONE of the ancient tyrants who was violently opposed to magicians, gypsies, fortune tellers and the like, observed a man who pretended to be a fortune teller, delivering some of his predictions to the crowd that surrounded him, and took the following method to shew his subjects the folly of such proceedings. After desiring the fortune-teller to answer a number of questions respecting the success of one of his intended expeditions, he asked him if he knew in what manner he himself should die? The fortune-teller, after some mystical examination, replied, "I shall die, may it please your majesty, in a fever." The tyrant to convince him not only of the fallibility, but the falsehood of his predictions, ordered the affrighted fortune teller to be executed directly—and after he had accompanied him to the place of execution in order to see the issue of his experiment, when the solemnity of the scene and idea of immediate death had thrown the poor creature into unusual agitation, asked him, "well, what think you of your prediction now?" The fortune-teller, requesting him to feel his pulse, replied "Did I not tell your majesty I should die in a fever?" The tyrant was so pleased with the ingenuity of the answer, and the feeling manner in which it was uttered, that he instantly pardoned him.

## General Advertiser, Philadelphia, Pennsylvania, July 16, 1793, pg. 3.

July 3.

We are favored with the following particulars of a transaction which happened in this city a few days past, viz. A negro woman, the property of Mr. Hutchins, schoolmaster, in this city, had pretended to have dreamed successively for two weeks, that several large chests of money were buried in her master's cellar: she accordingly communicated her dreams to a fortune-teller this fortune-teller laid a scheme with four others, to secrete themselves in the cellar, and dig for the supposed hidden treasure; accordingly, on Saturday evening last they contrived to get secreted in the cellar, and to work they went, with such secrecy and silence as not to be discovered until Sunday evening, at 5 o'clock, having been hard at work for near 48 hours; most providentially just in time to prevent the whole bui'ding [building] (a three story house) from falling in the whole and crushing to death not only themselves, but the whole family consisting of several persons.

We are favored with the following particulars of a tranfaction which happened in this city a few days paft. viz. A negro woman, the property of Mr. Hutchins, fchoolmafter, in this city, had pretended to have dreamed fucceffively for two weeks, that feveral large chefts of money were buried in her mafter's cellar: fhe accordingly communicated her dreams to a fortune-teller: this fortune-teller laid a fcheme with four others, to fecrete themfelves in the cellar, and dig for this fuppofed hidden treafure; accordingly, on Saturday evening laft they contrived to get fecreted in the cellar, and to work they went, with fuch fecrecy and filence as not to be difcovered until Sunday evening, at 5 o'clock, having been hard at work for near 48 hours; moft providentially juft in time to prevent the whole building (a three ftory houfe) from falling in and crufhing to death not only themfelves, but the whole family confifting of feveral perfons.

July 3.

They had dug twelve feet into, and under several parts of the foundation. Upon the examination of the negroes, before Benjamin Legare, Esq. J. P., it appears that they were possessed of a most strange infatuation; and they pretended to the spirit of divination, possessing the power of pre-knowledge, &

c. They were committed for examination and trial before a court of justice and freeholders.

"The above negroes, with three others, who are since discovered to have been concerned, were tried the 1st instant, before John Troup & Benjamin Legare, Esqrs. justices of the peace, and five freeholders; when six were brought in guilty, and were sentenced to 25 lashes each. Two were acquainted, having proved to have been deluded by the others."

# *The Maryland Gazette,* Annapolis, Maryland, August 3, 1797, pg. 3.

*Wonderful deceptions of Electricity*

Also a variety of novel entertainments by Mr. Salenka and the Dog,[79] never performed in this city; in particular the Dog, in character of a Fortune-teller, will tell any lady of gentleman's fortune by looking in their hands.

---

[79] Gabriel Salenka and his dog toured the nation preforming in theatres as a novelty act.

# Michelle Hamilton

# Chapter IV

## Conjurers

In the 18th-century, the term "conjuror" was used to describe a magician. Besides preforming sleight of hand tricks, conjurors also told fortunes as part of their repertoire. Like fortune tellers, conjurors were also considered by many to be charlatans and as the following articles highlight, they were frequently accused of cheating the unsuspecting out of considerable sums of money.

## *The Pennsylvania Gazette*, Philadelphia, Pennsylvania, April 22-29, 1731, pg. 3.

*Feb.* 20.

They write from *Montaguie* in *Normandie*, the 4th Instant, that about the Close of last Year, there happened a tragical Accident in a Village near that place, occasioned by the too great Credulity of the People in Witchcraft and Enchantment. A Man of that Village had been long ill of a

Distemper that baffled the Art of Physick; whereupon his Wife would have it that he was bewitched, and went to consult a pretended Conjurer who lived a few Leagues off. After he had asked her several Questions, he pretended to shew her the Wizard in a Glass of Water, who was her Husband's Uncle; and told her, they must force him to withdraw the Charm by beating him, and burning the Soles of his Feet. When she came home, she told her Relations what had passed, and desired them to come to her House and assist her in the Execution. She sent for her Husband's Uncle, and they beat the poor Man unmercifully, notwithstanding all his Protestations of Innocence, and burnt the Soles of his Feet and Crown of his Head with a red-hot Fire-shovel; and when they had done, they carried him home, where he lay in Torture two Days, and then died, having received all the Sacraments. The chief Magistrate of *Montagnie* hearing of it, ordered the Body to be taken up and searched; when the Marks of his barbarous Usage were but too visible. Upon this, the Provost ordered the Wife and all her Accomplices to be seized; and the Woman not only declared the whole Truth, but said, *If it was to do again, she would do it.*

## *The Pennsylvania Gazette,* Philadelphia, Pennsylvania, July 3, 1766, pg. 4.

Anti-Etam Forge, Frederick County, April 27.

RUN away from the above forge,[80] on the 20th instant, a servant man, named Thomas Mcclene, or Onan, an Irishman (tho' he says he is a Highlandman) a low squat fellow, of a

---

[80] Antietam Forge, also called Antietam Furnace in some records, made tacks and nails.

very swarthy complexion, with short black hair; he had on, when he went away, a blue cloth coat, a double-breasted jacket, of an ash-coloured bearskin cloth, trimmed with white flat metal buttons, a pair of buckskin breeches, old shoes, and a pair of grey milled, or worsted stockings. He commonly wears his garters under his knees, is a very talkative fellow, and pretends to be a conjurer, and brags much of his land and Negroes in Cecil or Kent county. Whoever brings, or secures the said fellow, so as I may have him again, shall receive THREE POUNDS Pennsylvania Currency, from

SAMUEL BEALL, jun.[81] for Self and Co.

N. B. He served some of his time about Darby, in Chester county, I believe, with one of the Smiths; and he has another man's wife with him.

*The Conjurers 1753.*

---

[81] Samuel Beall (1706-1780).

# Michelle Hamilton

## The Pennsylvania Packet, Philadelphia, Pennsylvania, November 18, 1771, pg. 3.

We hear, an eminent innholder in this city, bought lately a ticket in a certain lottery; and being determined to secure good luck to himself, went to consult a conjurer, whether the ticket was a fortunate or unfortunate one. In order to try the wizard's skill, the adventurer previously proposed, that he should tell him of which hundred the number of his ticket was, which the conjurer happily guessing, the innholder rejoicing, now thought, he could not fail of knowing whether his ticket would draw a prize or not; consequently he shewed his ticket, when it was condemned by the magician as unfortunate; whereupon, the possessor went to the gentleman, of whom he had bought the ticket, to change it for a fortunate one, who, not being of the same belief as the host, very readily complied with his request; and behold, a few days ago, the ticket, condemned by the conjurer, as unfortunate, came up with seven hundred pounds, and the ticket the innholder had got in exchange was a blank. The poor deceived man has been advised to sue the conjurer for damages; but we do not hear yet what method he will take to recover his loss.

*A late 18th-century Conjurer.*

# *The Pennsylvania Packet,* Philadelphia, Pennsylvania, June 21, 1790, pg. 2.s

*ASTROLOGY.*

WE have seen, in late European papers, accounts of two amiable young women having committed suicide, after having their *fortunes told,* by those idle pests to society, *fortune tellers.*—Louis XV,[82] rewarded the *ingenuity* of one of these *gentry,* in a manner which, if any thing can, makes despotism wear *some marks of justice.* An *astrologer,* just before the battle

---

[82] Louis XV of France (1710-1774) was King of France from 1715 to his death in 1774.

of *Fontenoy*,[83] made a violent effort to get into the presence of the king, to inform him of something of great importance—when there, he told the king his profession—and that from it he had knowledge that the king would die on such a day. This struck a panic in several of the courtiers and attendants on his Majesty; but the King, with perfect *sang froid* , asked the conjurer if he could tell the hour? The conjurer confessed that that was beyond his art: *then,* rejoined the king, *you are not so good an* astrologer *as I am; for I can tell you, that you will die this afternoon, precisely at five o'clock;* and immediately ordered that he should at that time be hanged. Events proved the conjurer a liar.

---

[83] The Battle of Fontenoy was fought on May 11, 1745 as part of the War of Austrian Succession. French forces won a decisive victory against the combined forces of the Dutch Republic, Great Britain, Hanover, and the Holy Roman Empire

# Chapter V

*Divination*

Divination is the act of seeing into the future using items such as a crystal ball, water, and smoke. In the following article, slaves in the West Indies island of Dominica used divination to commit resistance against their white owners.

## The Freeman's Journal or The North-American Intelligencer, Philadelphia, Pennsylvania, July 25, 1787, pg. 3.

ROSEAU, (Dominica) *May* 30.

On Sunday last (pursuant to the sentence pronounced by a bench of his majesty's justices of the peace) was inflicted the first part of the punishment, (*viz. thirty-nine* lashes) in the public market place of this town, on the negro *Cato*, commonly known in the quarter of Coulihaut, by the name of *Daddy*, the property of, or formerly belonging to Dr. Clifton, of the island of St. Christopher's. His crime was that of pretending to divination, or, as it is termed by the negroes, of possessing to be an *Obeah Man;*[84] under which character, he committed many enormities. He is, by his sentence, to receive the same punishment for three successive Sundays: the first part of which was inflicted last Sunday, above mentioned.

Jack receiving Obi.

*An Obeah ritual.*

This notorious rascal had the art to persuade numbers of people of his actually being gifted with the power which asserted he was possessed of:—(even several whites were weak enough to give way to the imposture). He, however, unfortunately for himself, could not see, that the time was come, when he was to be made a striking example, to deter similar rascals from practicing like impositions,—or he would have withdrawn himself from the hand of justice in time.

---

[84] Obeah was spiritual and healing practice that was practiced in the 18th-century by enslaved West Africans in the West Indies. The Obeah Man was the spiritual leader who encouraged his followers to preform acts of resistance and rebellion against white slaveholders.

# Chapter VI

## Necromancy

Necromancy was a form of fortune telling where the dead where summoned to predict the future. Like all forms of fortune telling documented in this book, the practice of necromancy was controversial, and practitioners were accused of being charlatans.

## *The Virginia Gazette,* Williamsburg, Virginia, June 18, 1772, pg. 2.

*Intelligence from the Publick Office, Bow Street.*[85]

Sarah Price, and Anne Wells (two of the finest and simplest Girls that Nature ever formed) charged William Anderson with extorting Money from them, under Pretence of helping them to Husbands by the Arts of Necromancy. Price had given at least ten Pounds, at different Times, to

---

[85] London's Bow Street Magistrates' Court.

Anderson or his Wife for Advice, Spells, and Charms, which Charms were sewed up in her under Petticoat. She had likewise given her a Note for three Hundred Pounds, payable after Marriage; but a Note for twenty Pounds was produced, which she declared on Oath she did not give. This gave Rise to a Suspicion that Anderson had forged the Girl's Mark, for she cannot write. Anderson's Wife acted the dumb Woman, wrote her Prophecies, and the Husband explained them to the Dupes of their Artifice. Another singular Circumstances in Anderson's Story is, that he was transported three Years since by the Name of William Williams; and the Transport Vessel being cast away, the Prisoners swam on Shore.

## *Gazette of the United-States,* Philadelphia, Pennsylvania, October 14, 1789, pg.

*Extract of a letter from Fayette-Ville, North Carolina dated September* 12.

What a spirit of free enquiry pervades the United States! a universal toleration in matters of religious opinion has done more to unfetter the human mind in a few years, than whole centuries of bigotry and superstition—That flood of light which poured in upon the world, when the press began to send forth its treasures, illuminated mankind to an astonishing degree, and raised human nature from the most abject depression, to a rank in the scale of being hitherto unknown.—This roused the powers of darkness; but the throne of ignorance being shaken to the centre, down fell the whole system of scholastic mummery, priestcraft, and false philosophy, which had been establishing itself for ages on the ruins of common sense, and public happiness—witchcraft, necromancy, juggling, and judicial astrology, which not a century since formed no inconsiderable part of the creed of the world, are now found without a meaning: Much however remains to be done. In America, we trust the human mind will have fair play—and that every species of false philosophy, false religion, and false government, will flee before the light of reason, and the dictates of common sense.

*Extract of a letter from Fayette-Ville, North-Carolina, dated September 12.*

" I think there is not a doubt that the Convention which is to meet here in November, will adopt the Constitution—the amendments will do the business.

" The season has been remarkably forward.— Flax-seed began to be brought in so early as July. —The crops of tobacco and wheat are very great.

" This State is settled by persons from all quarters, and many who come from the eastward fall victims to the climate, but then it is more owing to their own folly—they take care of themselves for a time, and then fall off to intemperance, which soon puts them under ground.—Four young men have died martyrs to rum, within a little while."

# Chapter VII

## Vampires

The belief in vampires, like witches and ghosts, have its roots in the ancient world. The ancient Greeks, Hebrews, and Chinese, among other cultures told stories about a demon like creature that is considered by scholars to be the forerunner of the vampire. In every version of the vampire legend, the creature was viewed as something that was feared for its ability to suck the life essence out of its victim. It is only recently that the vampire has become a romantic creature.

Hunting Vampires

## THE  Numb. 115,

# VIRGINIA GAZETTE.

*Containing the freſheſt Advices, Foreign and Domeſtick.*

From Friday, October 6, to Friday, October 13, 1738.

## *The Virginia Gazette,* Williamsburg, Virginia, October 6-13, 1738, pg. 3.

*Vienna, June* 21.

Letters from Temeswaer [Timişoara, Romania] [86] say, that the ridiculous Opinion of Vampires, which was so much talk'd [talked] of four or five Years ago, is again reviv'd [revived]. The common People's Notion of Vampires is this, that dead Bodies rise out of their Graves and suck the Blood of People asleep; after which they conclude, that the Persons suck'd [sucked] become in their turn Vampires; and to prevent any ill Effects from Bodies that are suspected to be of this Sort, they drive a Stake through the Heart, and cut off the Head. These superstitious Follies are suppos'd [supposed] to arise not only from the Ignorance of the Inhabitants of the Bannat, but to the Calamities it at present suffers, which occasions Panicks to prevail.

Letters from Temeſwaer ſay, that the rediculous Opinion of Vampires, which was ſo much talk'd of four or five Years ago, is again reviv'd. The common People's Notion of Vampires is this, that dead Bodies riſe out of their Graves and ſuck the Blood of People aſleep; after which they conclude, that the Perſons ſuck'd become in their turn Vampires; and to prevent any ill Effects from Bodies that are ſuſpected to be of this Sort, they drive a Stake through the Heart, and cut off the Head. Theſe ſuperſtitious Follies are ſuppos'd to ariſe not only from the Ignorance of the Inhabitants of the Bannat, but to the Calamities it at preſent ſuffers, which occaſions Panicks to prevail.

---

[86] In 1738, the city of Timişoara was part of the Kingdom of Hungary.

Michelle Hamilton

# About the Author

Michelle L. Hamilton earned her master's degree in history from San Diego State University in 2013. In her free time, Michelle is a Civil War and 18th-century living historian. Born and raised in California, Michelle now resides in Ruther Glen, Virginia. Michelle is the author of *"I Would Still Be Drowned in Tears": Spiritualism in Abraham Lincoln's White House*, and *Civil War Ghosts*.

You can follow her at her blog:
http://michelle-hamilton.blogspot.com.

Another Haunted Road Media title from Michelle Hamilton:

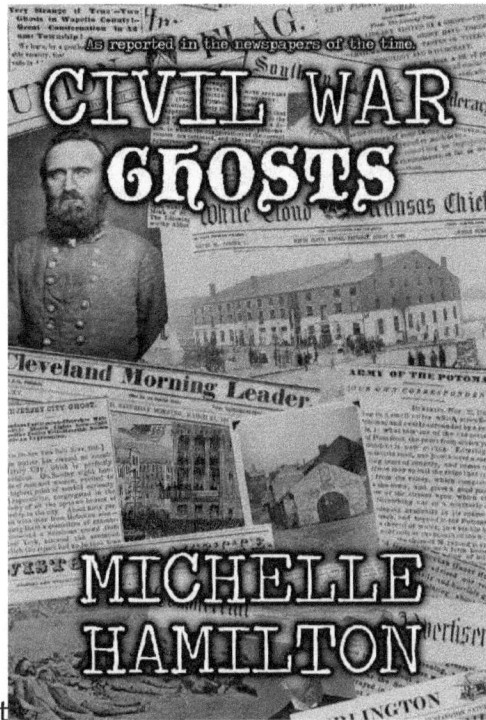

While the War Between The States raged, the country's spirits were restless... Civil War Ghosts takes a look inside real ghost stories reported at the time of the Civil War. Covering each year from 1860 - 1865, explore real newspaper articles that weren't afraid to write about paranormal activity happening throughout the country during a time of national upheaval. Civil War Ghosts is a unique supernatural look at America while the states battled each other.

# Michelle Hamilton

For more information visit:
www.hauntedroadmedia.com